Otto Amaro

Dark Psychology Secrets
Techniques and Strategies for Navigating Human Behavior

Original title: Segredos da Psicologia Sombria

Copyright © 2024, published by Luiz Antonio dos Santos ME.

This book is a non-fiction work that explores advanced techniques and strategies in the field of dark psychology. Through a detailed analysis of psychological and behavioral concepts, the author offers practical tools to understand and navigate human behavior, maintaining an ethical and responsible approach.

1st Edition

Production Team
Author: Otto Amaro
Editor: Luiz Santos
Revision: Anselmo Mendes
Cover: Studios Booklas / Amadeu Rossi
Layout: Roger Dumas
Translator: Raul Smith

Publication and Identification
ISBN: 978-65-9981-023-7
Dark Psychology Secrets / By Otto Amaro

Editora Booklas, 2024
Categories: Psychology / Self-Development / Human Behavior
DDC: 158.9 - CDU: 159.9

All rights reserved to:
Luiz Antonio dos Santos ME / Booklas
No part of this book may be reproduced, stored in a retrieval system, or transmitted by any means - electronic, mechanical, photocopying, recording, or otherwise - without 1 the prior and express permission of the copyright 2 holder.

Summary

Prologue 5
Chapter 1 Introduction to the Topic 7
Chapter 2 Origins and Historical Context 11
Chapter 3 Understanding Human Behavior 15
Chapter 4 The Nature of Persuasion 19
Chapter 5 The Power of Communication 23
Chapter 6 The Art of Reading People 27
Chapter 7 Emotions and Decision-Making 31
Chapter 8 Introduction to Manipulation 35
Chapter 9 Common Manipulation Techniques 39
Chapter 10 The Psychology of Fear 43
Chapter 11 Creating Rapport 47
Chapter 12 Mirroring Techniques 51
Chapter 13 Beliefs and Convictions 55
Chapter 14 Identifying Weaknesses 59
Chapter 15 The Psychology of Authority 64
Chapter 16 Negotiation Techniques 68
Chapter 17 The Power of Suggestion 73
Chapter 18 Conflict Management 78
Chapter 19 Group Behavior 83
Chapter 20 Building Credibility 88
Chapter 21 Storytelling Techniques 93
Chapter 22 Manipulating Perceptions 98
Chapter 23 Introduction to Gaslighting 103

Chapter 24 The Art of Distraction 107
Chapter 25 Planting Ideas 112
Chapter 26 Creating Dependency 116
Chapter 27 Recognizing Manipulators 121
Chapter 28 The Role of Reverse Psychology 126
Chapter 29 Dealing with Resistance 131
Chapter 30 The Power of Silence 136
Chapter 31 Subtle Intimidation 140
Chapter 32 The Psychology of Reciprocity 145
Chapter 33 Recognizing Falsehoods 149
Chapter 34 The Importance of Timing 154
Chapter 35 Creating Scarcity 159
Chapter 36 Behavior Modeling 164
Chapter 37 Introduction to Conversational Hypnosis 169
Chapter 38 Advanced Emotional Control 174
Chapter 39 Dealing with Criticism 179
Chapter 40 Using Rewards 184
Chapter 41 Narrative Control 189
Chapter 42 Advanced Social Manipulation 194
Chapter 43 Protecting Yourself from Manipulation 199
Chapter 44 Dark Psychology at Work 204
Chapter 45 Influence on Social Media 209
Chapter 46 Creating Magnetic Charisma 214
Chapter 47 Seduction Techniques 219
Chapter 48 Impression Management 224
Chapter 49 Psychology in Financial Decisions 229
Chapter 50 Mass Influence 234

Chapter 51 Developing Mental Resilience 239
Chapter 52 Long-Term Strategies.. 243
Chapter 53 Ethics in Dark Psychology 248
Chapter 54 Case Studies 253
Chapter 55 Practices and Exercises 258
Chapter 56 Conclusion and Next Steps.................................... 263
Epilogue 267

Prologue

You hold in your hands a map. Not a typical map with streets and predictable destinations, but a guide that penetrates the intricate cartography of the human mind. This book is a key, a portal to a world where choices are not just made, but shaped, and where interactions are not just experienced, but strategically designed. Here, you will find a unique power, both fascinating and disturbing: the power to understand human behavior in its deepest layers and to use it in a transformative way.

Have you ever wondered why some people always seem to be in control? How certain individuals manage to influence crowds, close improbable deals, or win anyone's trust, while others struggle to be heard? There is a code, a hidden mechanism behind decisions, emotions, and behaviors. It is not visible on the surface, but when discovered, it reveals a new way of seeing the world and the relationships that define us.

At this very moment, you are about to unravel that code. Dark psychology is not an esoteric concept, reserved for experts or unscrupulous manipulators. It is a skill, a science, and above all, a lens. Through it, every conversation, every gesture, and every choice can be understood in ways that previously seemed impossible.

Here, there are no empty promises or easy shortcuts. This is a call to awareness, an invitation for you to take control of your own narrative. The knowledge offered is not to be used against others, but to protect yourself and those you love. Understanding the mechanisms of manipulation, persuasion, and emotional control is not just a matter of strategy, but of survival in a world where external influences try to shape who you are.

As you progress, you will be challenged to question what you know about freedom, choices, and authenticity. With each page, you will be confronted with truths that may initially seem uncomfortable but have the potential to set you free. After all, as a wise man once said: "Knowledge is power." But not just any knowledge. Only the one that makes you aware of your strength and your vulnerabilities.

Allow yourself to immerse yourself in this universe. It's not just about learning; it's about seeing, feeling, and understanding as never before. This book is your mirror and your window, showing who you are and what the world around you really means. By crossing this threshold, you will no longer be the same. The journey begins now.

Luiz Santos
Editor

Chapter 1
Introduction to the Topic

Dark psychology, a fascinating and often misunderstood field, emerges as a powerful lens for understanding the complexities of human behavior and the dynamics of influence. When unveiled, it reveals techniques and concepts that, when used consciously, can both protect and empower individuals to navigate a world of constant social and emotional interactions.

The essence of dark psychology lies in the understanding and manipulation of people's mental and behavioral processes. It is an approach that goes beyond the conventional study of the human mind, exploring the mechanisms that make it possible to persuade, influence, or, in extreme cases, manipulate the choices of others. This practice, however, is not intrinsically evil. Ethical judgment rests on the practitioner's intentions and the effects of their actions.

Ethical and Unethical Manipulation

Manipulation, in the context of dark psychology, is not a homogeneous entity. Divided between the ethical and unethical poles, it presents itself in different ways. Ethical manipulation is one that respects the limits and consent of the other, used to facilitate decisions or create harmony in social situations. On the other hand, unethical manipulation disregards the well-being of others, using tricks that can emotionally or psychologically harm a person.

A simple example of ethical manipulation would be using dark psychology to help a friend overcome a self-sabotaging belief. By highlighting their strengths and softening their fears, you guide them to a more positive choice. An unethical example would be emotionally manipulating someone for personal gain, ignoring the consequences for the victim.

Everyday Applications

Dark psychology permeates our daily lives in subtle ways. From advertising campaigns that lead us to desire the latest technological device to social interactions where, consciously or unconsciously, we adjust our behavior to gain empathy, respect, or cooperation.

Imagine a scenario where someone uses body language and carefully chosen words to persuade a group in a meeting. The choice of strategic pauses, confident eye contact, and an assertive tone of voice are elements that influence decisions without participants consciously realizing the impact of these strategies.

On the other hand, dark psychology can be applied to protect oneself from external influences. Recognizing tactics such as gaslighting or emotional manipulation is crucial to setting boundaries and maintaining mental autonomy. Knowing how to identify when someone is trying to control your actions or decisions is as important as learning to influence others in a positive way.

Foundations for Responsible Knowledge

Entering this universe requires an open mind and a clear sense of responsibility. Knowledge of dark psychology techniques should not be seen as an invitation to selfish manipulation, but as a tool to expand your understanding of human behavior and enhance your communication and influence skills.

Throughout this book, the reader will find methods and strategies ranging from simple persuasion to more sophisticated techniques. Each approach will be explored in detail, with a solid ethical foundation, allowing you to understand both the positive impact and potential dangers of its application.

Protection and Positive Influence

Dark psychology, in its ethical application, offers a way to transform everyday interactions. In a negotiation, for example, it can help create a mutually beneficial relationship, while in an interpersonal relationship, it can strengthen bonds through more empathetic and aligned communication.

On the other hand, when the goal is protection, knowing common manipulation tactics helps to identify situations where your autonomy is being challenged. For example, by recognizing signs of microexpressions that reveal hidden intentions, you can anticipate a manipulator's moves before they have a chance to influence you.

A World of Possibilities

From this introduction, it becomes clear that dark psychology is not an instrument of destruction, but a key to unraveling the complexity of human relationships. Whether to protect yourself from negative influences or to conduct interactions more effectively, this field of study offers a rich and practical perspective.

The path through dark psychology begins with awareness. Becoming aware of the elements that influence thoughts, emotions, and behaviors is the first step to transformation. More than ever, understanding this topic opens doors to a more intentional and assertive existence, in which choices cease to be reactive and become strategic.

Thus, one enters the multifaceted universe of dark psychology, where each interaction hides layers of complexity and opportunity. It is time to explore what lies beyond the surface, revealing the forces that shape our connections, decisions, and ultimately, our lives.

Chapter 2
Origins and Historical Context

The history of dark psychology unfolds as a fascinating mosaic of philosophical contributions, scientific advances, and practical observations about human behavior. Its origins date back to ancient times when early thinkers began to explore the mysteries of the mind, the nature of social interactions, and the means by which people can be influenced or controlled. This chapter is a deep dive into the roots that underpin this enigmatic field, revealing the figures and theories that shaped its scientific and conceptual basis.

The Beginning: Philosophy and Rhetoric

The influence of dark psychology can be traced back to Ancient Greece, where philosophers like Socrates, Plato, and Aristotle initiated discussions about persuasion and the nature of power in human interactions. Aristotle, in particular, developed the concepts of logos, pathos, and ethos, pillars of rhetoric that still underpin the art of influencing and persuading today.

While logos refers to the appeal to logic and reason, pathos explores the manipulation of emotions, and ethos focuses on the credibility of the speaker. The combination of these techniques was widely used to shape public opinion in speeches and debates. These elements became essential tools for those seeking to control narratives and shape perceptions.

The Sophists, contemporaries of Aristotle, also played a crucial role. Masters of argumentation, they taught how to persuade, regardless of the morality or veracity of the argument, which generated intense debates about ethics in influence.

Evolution in the Psychological Field

Moving on to the 19th century, the emergence of psychology as a science brought new rigor to the study of human behavior. Sigmund Freud was a central figure, introducing psychoanalysis as an approach to understanding the unconscious. Freud argued that our repressed desires and internal conflicts profoundly influence our actions. Although he did not use the term "dark psychology," his ideas about manipulating the unconscious paved the way for many modern techniques.

Gustave Le Bon, a contemporary of Freud, focused on how crowds can be influenced. In his work "The Psychology of Crowds," Le Bon described how charismatic leaders manipulate groups using emotional appeals and exaggerated simplifications. His studies were later used for both benevolent purposes and authoritarian regimes, demonstrating the power of applying these ideas.

In the early 20th century, B.F. Skinner introduced the concept of operant conditioning, which became a practical tool for shaping behaviors. His experiments showed that positive and negative reinforcements could influence actions predictably, providing a scientific basis for many manipulation tactics used today.

Contributions of Cognitive Psychology

Advances in cognitive psychology, from the 1950s onwards, brought to light the cognitive biases and mental traps that we all face. Daniel Kahneman and Amos Tversky, in their research on decision-making, revealed how people often act irrationally, influenced by heuristics and distorted perceptions. These findings formed the basis for manipulation techniques that exploit our mental vulnerabilities, such as anchoring bias or the framing effect.

Simultaneously, Albert Bandura's research on social learning highlighted the importance of observation and imitation. Bandura demonstrated that human behavior is shaped not only by direct reinforcements but also by the influence of models and social patterns. This principle is widely used in advertising campaigns and modern social dynamics.

The Role of Culture and Politics

Dark psychology found fertile ground in cultural and political contexts, where the ideas of manipulation and persuasion were applied on a large scale. Totalitarian regimes, such as Adolf Hitler's, exploited Le Bon's teachings on mass psychology to consolidate power and influence entire populations.

During the Cold War, superpowers began investing in psychological control research, developing strategies to manipulate beliefs and behaviors in espionage and propaganda contexts. The CIA's Project MKUltra is a controversial example of how psychological manipulation was explored in depth.

Influence of Media and Technology

In the 20th and 21st centuries, the exponential growth of communication technologies brought new possibilities for the application of dark psychology. Mass media, social networks, and digital advertising began to use psychological insights to shape behaviors on a global scale.

Companies began to apply techniques such as FOMO (fear of missing out) and gamification to capture consumer attention and encourage them to act in specific ways. The use of algorithms to target personalized content amplified the effectiveness of these strategies, creating a new era of digital manipulation.

Ethics Throughout History

From the Sophists to modern marketing campaigns, the question of ethics has permeated the use of dark psychology. While some defend it as a neutral tool, whose impact depends on the intention of those who use it, others argue that its potential to cause harm requires greater regulation and awareness.

For example, manipulating perceptions through disinformation raises serious ethical dilemmas. Despite this, the same principles can be used to raise awareness among populations, promoting public health or education campaigns, demonstrating that the line between benefit and harm is often tenuous.

A Foundation for the Present

Understanding the historical context of dark psychology is essential to appreciating its evolution and complexity. The foundations established by philosophers, scientists, and social observers continue to influence contemporary practices, providing a solid basis for exploring the techniques and strategies that unfold in the following chapters.

This historical overview not only illuminates the paths already traveled but also sheds light on the opportunities and risks that accompany the use of this knowledge. As in its beginning, dark psychology remains a powerful tool, available to those who wish to decipher the enigmas of the human mind and shape interactions in their own reality.

Chapter 3
Understanding Human Behavior

The key to unraveling the intricate webs of human behavior lies in understanding the mental and emotional processes that drive people's decisions and actions. Every choice, however simple it may seem, is shaped by a combination of psychological, emotional, and social factors. This chapter explores the fundamentals of behavioral psychology, highlighting the crucial elements that govern human choices and introducing essential concepts for the study of dark psychology.

The Decision-Making Machine

Human behavior is the result of an intricate internal processing system. The human brain constantly evaluates available information, weighing risks, benefits, and emotional contexts. However, decision-making is not a purely logical process. In fact, it is deeply influenced by emotions, past experiences, and cognitive biases.

Research shows that decisions are often made automatically, based on mental shortcuts known as heuristics. These shortcuts help the brain save energy but often lead to quick and irrational judgments. For example, the representativeness heuristic causes people to assess a situation based on its similarity to familiar prototypes, ignoring other relevant information.

The Role of Emotions

Emotions play a central role in human behavior, often outweighing logic in the hierarchy of priorities. Studies indicate that important decisions, such as choosing a partner, accepting a job offer, or buying a product, are strongly influenced by the emotional state at the time of choice.

For example, anchoring bias can be amplified by emotions. In a negotiation scenario, a strategic initial offer creates an emotional anchor that influences subsequent perceptions, even if logic suggests a different outcome. The impact of emotional state on interpreting and responding to this anchor demonstrates how emotions shape our choices.

Cognitive Biases: The Mental Trap

Cognitive biases are systematic distortions in reasoning that affect how we interpret information and make decisions. These are some of the most relevant to dark psychology:

Confirmation bias: The tendency to seek or value information that confirms our existing beliefs, ignoring contradictory data.

Availability bias: The disproportionate weight given to information that is most readily available in our memory, often influenced by recent or impactful events.

Halo effect: The positive or negative perception of a single trait of a person or situation influences the evaluation of other related aspects.

Understanding these biases allows you to manipulate perceptions and decisions effectively. By presenting information selectively or highlighting specific aspects of a situation, it is possible to influence the conclusions people draw.

Conditioning: The Basis of Learned Behavior

Human behavior is also shaped by conditioning, mechanisms that reinforce or inhibit actions based on their consequences. The two main types of conditioning are:

Classical conditioning: Introduced by Ivan Pavlov, it occurs when an automatic response is associated with a previously neutral stimulus. For example, a brand can create positive associations with happiness and success in its advertising campaigns, subconsciously influencing consumers to prefer its products.

Operant conditioning: Proposed by B.F. Skinner, it is based on reinforcement or punishment. Positive reinforcements encourage a behavior by providing rewards, while negative reinforcements encourage it by removing unpleasant stimuli. On the other hand, punishments reduce the likelihood of a behavior being repeated.

These principles are widely used in marketing and motivation strategies, from loyalty programs to gamification systems.

Social Dynamics and External Pressures

In addition to internal processes, human behavior is deeply influenced by the social environment. Norms, expectations, and group dynamics shape our choices and actions. Phenomena such as conformity and social pressure demonstrate how the desire to belong can override individual convictions.

Solomon Asch's famous experiment revealed that, in group situations, people often give in to the majority, even when they know the majority is wrong. This principle is exploited in mass persuasion campaigns and social manipulations, where creating a "majority opinion" can influence individual behaviors.

Practical Applications: Exploring Behavior

The ability to understand the fundamentals of human behavior opens doors to countless practical possibilities:

Identify vulnerabilities: By observing behavioral patterns, it is possible to anticipate reactions and exploit a person's emotional or cognitive vulnerabilities.

Adapt strategies: Adjusting the communication or negotiation approach based on an individual's emotional triggers and cognitive biases increases the effectiveness of interactions.

Protect yourself: Recognizing biases in yourself or others helps to avoid external manipulations.

Deciphering the Unconscious

Behind conscious behavior, the unconscious plays a crucial role. Research suggests that most of our decisions are made before we are even aware of them. The unconscious processes environmental stimuli and emotional memories to influence our judgments.

This characteristic is exploited in influencing techniques, such as subliminal messages and indirect suggestions. One example is how carefully designed scenarios in stores—including lighting, music, and fragrances—stimulate the senses to create a positive emotional experience and encourage impulsive purchases.

Building Knowledge

By understanding the factors that shape human behavior, you not only decipher the mysteries behind people's actions but also acquire tools to influence them more effectively. This is a fundamental step in the journey through dark psychology, as it lays the foundation for the more advanced techniques and strategies that will be explored in the following chapters.

Human choices are neither random nor purely rational. They are woven into a tangle of emotions, logic, and external influences. Understanding this complexity not only offers valuable insights but also positions you as a more conscious observer and participant in the intricate theater of human interactions.

Chapter 4
The Nature of Persuasion

Persuasion is a powerful force, an invisible thread that connects people, shapes decisions, and transforms behaviors. Unlike manipulation, which often acts in a sneaky and exploitative way, persuasion can be a balanced tool, respecting the autonomy of the receiver. This chapter reveals the fundamentals of persuasion, its essential principles, and the forms of practical application in everyday life, highlighting how it differs from manipulation and why understanding this dynamic is essential to exploring the vast territory of dark psychology.

What is Persuasion?

To persuade is more than to convince; it is to directly influence someone's beliefs, attitudes, or behaviors through arguments, communication, and emotional connection. Persuasion involves a subtle interplay between logic and emotion, exploring the desires, fears, and values of the person to be influenced.

Aristotle, one of the first to theorize about persuasion, defined its three pillars:

Ethos: The credibility of the speaker. The more trustworthy, experienced, or charismatic you appear, the greater the impact of your message.

Pathos: The emotional connection. To persuade, it is crucial to touch the other person's emotions, creating empathy and awakening feelings that reinforce your argument.

Logos: The appeal to logic and reason. Well-structured arguments backed by facts make your ideas more convincing.

These principles form the basis of modern persuasion but have been expanded by decades of research in psychology and human behavior.

Basic Principles of Persuasion

Psychologist Robert Cialdini, in his influential work on persuasion, presented six fundamental principles that govern how people are influenced:

Reciprocity: People have a strong tendency to reciprocate favors or gestures. A generous act can create an implicit obligation to reciprocate.

Commitment and consistency: Once someone makes a commitment, they are more likely to continue acting consistently with it, even if doubts arise.

Social proof: People tend to follow the actions of others, especially in situations of uncertainty. Showing that others approve of or adhere to an idea increases its persuasiveness.

Liking: We are more likely to be persuaded by people we like or with whom we identify.

Authority: The perception that someone is an authority figure increases the credibility of their message.

Scarcity: The feeling that something is limited or exclusive increases its perceived value and the desire to obtain it.

These principles are widely used in negotiations, marketing, interpersonal relationships, and even politics, creating a practical foundation for persuasion in everyday life.

Persuasion in Everyday Life

Examples of persuasion are everywhere. A salesperson who points out that "only a few units" of a product are available is using the principle of scarcity. A digital influencer who shares testimonials from satisfied customers uses social proof to validate a service.

In a personal context, persuasion can occur in simple interactions, such as convincing a friend to adopt a new idea. The choice of words, tone of voice, and even body language play crucial roles.

Imagine a scenario where you need to persuade a colleague to collaborate on a project. Presenting clear and reasonable arguments (logos), demonstrating enthusiasm and empathy (pathos), and establishing your competence and good intentions (ethos) will significantly increase your chances of success.

Persuasion Versus Manipulation

The line between persuasion and manipulation can be thin, but it is important to distinguish them. While persuasion operates within ethical limits, respecting the other person's freedom of choice, manipulation aims to control or exploit, often without regard for the negative impact.

For example, persuading a customer to purchase a product by showing its real benefits is ethical. Manipulating them through false information or playing on their fears would be unethical. This difference lies in the intention and transparency of the approach.

Practical Persuasion Strategies

To apply persuasion effectively and ethically, some strategies are essential:

Build rapport: Relate authentically and create common ground. Trust is the foundation of any persuasive interaction.

Focus on benefits: Instead of just listing features, highlight how your proposal can directly benefit the other person.

Tell stories: Captivating stories evoke emotions and make it easier to connect with your message.

Personalize your approach: Understand the interests, values, and motivations of the person you want to persuade and tailor your message to those elements.

Use body language: Open posture, eye contact, and congruent gestures increase your credibility and impact.

These techniques not only make your communication more effective but also help build stronger and more meaningful relationships.

Exploring the Limits of Persuasion

While persuasion can be a positive tool, it also presents challenges. It is essential to be aware of ethical limits and the possibility of resistance. Persuasion should be a fair exchange where both parties have the autonomy to accept or refuse.

In situations of resistance, an indirect approach may be more effective. Instead of confronting directly, introduce ideas gradually, allowing the person to feel in control of their choices. Techniques such as the foot-in-the-door effect—starting with a small request to increase the likelihood of acceptance of a larger one later—are practical examples of this approach.

The Impact of Persuasion on Personal Development

Mastering the art of persuasion is not just a social skill; it is also a form of self-empowerment. By learning to influence effectively, you gain confidence in your interactions and improve your ability to achieve goals.

Furthermore, understanding the mechanisms of persuasion allows you to recognize when someone is trying to influence you. This knowledge is a powerful form of protection against unethical manipulations, helping you maintain your autonomy.

The Role of Persuasion in Dark Psychology

Within the context of dark psychology, persuasion is a fundamental tool. It is the gateway to more advanced techniques such as reading behaviors, emotional manipulation, and narrative control. Understanding its nature and application is the first step to mastering more complex strategies that shape human interactions.

Persuasion, contrary to what many believe, is not an art reserved for skilled speakers or manipulators. It is a skill that everyone can develop, transforming everyday interactions into opportunities to create impact, resolve conflicts, and build deeper connections.

Chapter 5
The Power of Communication

Communication is the foundation of all human interaction, an invisible bridge that connects thoughts, emotions, and intentions between individuals. Although often considered merely the act of speaking and listening, communication is a much deeper phenomenon, composed of verbal language, non-verbal cues, and emotional subtleties. This chapter reveals how communication can be used to influence and shape human behavior, exploring the nuances of tone of voice, body language, and word choice, as well as presenting practical strategies to enhance your communication skills.

Communication as a Tool of Influence

The power of communication lies in its ability to transcend barriers and affect the subconscious. It is not just about transmitting a message, but about creating a shared experience that resonates emotionally with the receiver. In a world where words can inspire, persuade, or manipulate, mastering the art of communication becomes an indispensable skill.

The science of effective communication begins with the understanding that what you say is important, but how you say it can be even more impactful. Studies show that about 93% of interpersonal communication is composed of non-verbal aspects, including body language and tone of voice. Words are the skeleton of the message; tone and gestures are the flesh and blood that bring it to life.

Body Language: What is Not Said

Body language is the most primitive form of communication. Even before words are spoken, our bodies transmit signals that can reveal intentions, emotions, and attitudes.

The most significant aspects of body language include:

Posture: An upright posture demonstrates confidence, while slumped shoulders or a withdrawn posture can indicate insecurity.

Eye contact: Looking directly into the interlocutor's eyes creates a sense of connection and trust. However, avoiding or exaggerating eye contact can generate distrust or discomfort.

Gestures: Smooth and congruent movements reinforce the verbal message. Excessive or disconnected gestures can distract or confuse.

Facial expressions: Microexpressions, which last only fractions of a second, often reveal true emotions before the person has a chance to mask them.

To improve perception and control of body language, the practice of observation is essential. Paying attention to the bodily reactions of others during a conversation helps to interpret hidden emotions, while adjusting your own body language can strengthen your presence and impact.

Tone of Voice: A Summoner of Emotions

Tone of voice is another critical element in communication. The same sentence can be interpreted in several ways depending on the intonation used. For example, a simple "Is everything okay?" can sound like a demonstration of empathy, a skeptical question, or even an expression of sarcasm.

Key elements of tone of voice include:

Volume: A balanced volume projects confidence, while a tone that is too loud or too low can indicate aggression or insecurity.

Pace: Speaking slowly with strategic pauses conveys clarity and authority, while a fast-paced speech can seem nervous or confusing.

Modulation: Varying intonation keeps the listener interested and helps emphasize important points.

Practicing voice modulation can make a significant difference. For example, when addressing a sensitive topic, a calm, low tone conveys care and understanding. In a presentation or negotiation, a more energetic and confident tone attracts attention and reinforces your message.

The Choice of Words

Although tone and body language are crucial, word choice also plays a vital role. Words have power, evoking images, emotions, and memories. Some tips to enhance the impact of your verbal language include:

Use positive words: Even in challenging situations, choose terms that inspire confidence and optimism. For example, say "We can improve this" instead of "This is wrong."

Be clear and direct: Complicated messages lose strength. Structure your ideas logically and avoid unnecessary jargon.

Appeal to the senses: Words that evoke sensory images, such as "warm," "soft," or "vibrant," create a deeper connection with the listener.

Assertive Communication: The Balance Between Empathy and Authority

Assertive communication is a skill that combines confidence and respect. It allows you to express your needs and opinions clearly, without disrespecting or aggressing the other person.

To communicate assertively:

Practice active listening: Show genuine interest in what the other person is saying, confirming your understanding with nods or questions.

Use "I" instead of "you": Statements like "I feel that..." are less accusatory than "You did this...".

Set boundaries: Be firm when communicating your limits, but avoid aggressive tones.

This approach balances rapport building with defending your own interests, making your interactions more productive and respectful.

Advanced Communication Strategies

Once the fundamentals are mastered, it is possible to explore more advanced techniques to influence and engage:

Mirroring: Subtly reproducing the interlocutor's body language or tone of voice creates empathy and comfort.

Metaphors and analogies: Using figures of speech facilitates the understanding of complex concepts and makes your message more memorable.

Open-ended questions: Encourage the other person to share more details, demonstrating interest and promoting a richer exchange.

For example, in a negotiation, a good communicator can start with subtle mirroring of the opponent's posture, use a metaphor to illustrate the benefits of their proposal, and conclude with open-ended questions that guide the conversation toward consensus.

The Role of Communication in Dark Psychology

In the context of dark psychology, communication is an essential tool for directing perceptions and emotions. Whether to build rapport, lead groups, or influence decisions, the way you communicate defines the impact of your interactions. Techniques such as adjusting tone, careful choice of words, and controlling body language become powerful weapons in the influencer's arsenal.

Communication as a Gateway

Mastering the power of communication is the first step to becoming a master of human interaction. With practice and attention to detail, each conversation ceases to be a simple exchange of words and becomes an opportunity for connection, influence, and transformation.

Mastery of communication is not just a practical skill; it is a portal to understanding the other on a deeper level, paving the way for more advanced applications and impact strategies that will be explored in the following chapters.

Chapter 6
The Art of Reading People

Reading people is a skill that transcends words, an ability to interpret the subtle cues people reveal in their actions, body language, and microexpressions. It is not about guesswork or vague intuition, but about careful and methodical observation, based on psychological and behavioral principles. This chapter unlocks the secrets of reading people, providing practical techniques to decipher hidden thoughts, intentions, and emotions, revealing what is often beyond the reach of words.

What is Reading People?

Reading people is the ability to capture and interpret nonverbal cues and behavioral patterns to understand their intentions, emotions, and motivations. It is a process of active observation that requires attention to detail and a thorough understanding of the signals that the body and face convey.

Contrary to popular belief, reading people is not an innate ability exclusive to some. It is a practice that can be learned and improved through study and experience. However, it requires patience, keen perception, and an open mind.

Body Language as a Mirror of the Mind

Body language is one of the richest sources of information about a person's emotional and mental state. Research shows that much of human communication is nonverbal, making observation of posture, gestures, and movements a powerful tool in reading people.

The main elements of body language include:

Posture: The way someone positions themselves can indicate confidence, insecurity, or discomfort. An upright posture suggests self-confidence, while slumped shoulders or withdrawn movements can reveal nervousness or submission.

Gestures: Hand and arm movements can reinforce or contradict the verbal message. For example, crossed arms can indicate defensiveness or discomfort, while open gestures suggest receptivity.

Physical distance: The proximity someone maintains during an interaction can reflect intimacy, trust, or, conversely, the need for space and boundaries.

Practicing observing these elements in everyday interactions is an effective way to develop your sensitivity to body language.

Microexpressions: Windows to the Truth

Microexpressions are quick and involuntary, often lasting only a fraction of a second. They appear when someone tries to suppress or conceal an emotion, revealing genuine feelings before consciousness takes over.

Identifying microexpressions requires attention and training. Among the most common emotions reflected are:

Anger: Lowered and furrowed eyebrows, pursed lips.

Joy: Narrowed eyes, wrinkles around the eyes, and a genuine smile.

Fear: Raised and drawn together eyebrows, wide eyes, slightly open mouth.

Contempt: One side of the lip raised, forming a unilateral smile.

Training in detecting microexpressions can be done with the help of videos, mirrors, or even in real interactions, paying attention to what is shown quickly before being replaced by a controlled expression.

Behavioral Patterns

In addition to facial expressions and body language, behavior patterns provide valuable clues. Some people have predictable ways of reacting in certain situations, and recognizing these patterns allows you to anticipate their actions.

Examples of behavioral patterns include:

Repetitive reactions: Someone who always avoids eye contact in times of pressure may be hiding something or feeling uncomfortable.

Sudden changes: Changes in tone of voice, posture, or speaking pace can indicate stress, lying, or intense emotion.

Social skills: Socially skilled people tend to mask signs of nervousness, but still let slip small clues.

The key to identifying behavioral patterns is to observe the person in different contexts and identify consistencies or deviations in their usual behavior.

Contextual Interpretation

Reading people is inseparable from context. A gesture that indicates nervousness in one setting may signify excitement in another. Thus, it is essential to consider the circumstances and environment before drawing conclusions.

For example, crossing your arms in a cold environment may be an attempt to warm up, while the same action in a meeting may reflect defensiveness or discomfort.

Another contextual aspect is the pre-existing relationship. Someone who feels comfortable with you may demonstrate more open behaviors, while a stranger may adopt a more reserved posture.

Practical Techniques for Reading People

Applying people-reading in everyday life requires practice and a set of specific techniques:

Observe without judging: Before interpreting, gather as much information as possible. Avoid jumping to conclusions, as signals can have different meanings depending on the context.

Pay attention to inconsistencies: When what is said contradicts what is shown, the truth usually lies in the nonverbal cues.

Use open-ended questions: Encourage the other person to share more information, allowing you to observe genuine reactions.

Study culture-based behaviors: Certain gestures or expressions may vary in meaning across different cultures. Understanding these nuances increases your accuracy in reading.

Practical Applications of Reading People

Reading people can be used in a wide range of situations:

Negotiations: Identifying signs of hesitation or interest helps to adjust your approach for better results.

Social interactions: Recognizing hidden emotions allows you to respond more empathetically and effectively.

Protection against manipulation: Detecting inconsistencies in behavior helps identify attempts at manipulation or deception.

For example, during a conversation, a slight twitch in someone's lips may indicate resistance or disagreement, even if their words are positive. Recognizing this cue allows you to adjust your message before resistance escalates.

Limitations and Ethics in Reading People

Although reading people is a powerful skill, it is not foolproof. Mistakes can occur due to personal biases or misinterpretations. Therefore, it is essential to use this skill as a tool for understanding and not for hasty judgment.

Furthermore, the ethical use of reading people is crucial. This skill should be used to improve communication and create more meaningful connections, never as a form of exploitation or unfair control.

The Connection to Dark Psychology

In dark psychology, reading people is a fundamental skill. It is the basis for more advanced techniques, such as persuasion, emotional manipulation, and social control. By understanding the cues that people unconsciously emit, you gain the ability to shape interactions subtly and effectively.

Reading people, at its core, is a celebration of human complexity. Deciphering the hidden messages in gestures, expressions, and behaviors is like unraveling a secret language, rich in nuances and meanings. With practice and ethical intent, this skill transforms the way you interact with the world, providing clarity, connection, and control.

Chapter 7
Emotions and Decision-Making

Emotions are the invisible forces that shape every human decision, acting as silent compasses that guide behaviors and choices. Often considered irrational, they play a crucial role in the decision-making process, influencing everything from the simplest to the most complex decisions. This chapter delves into the intimate relationship between emotions and choices, revealing how emotions can be controlled and manipulated to achieve specific goals.

The Role of Emotions in Decisions

Contrary to the common belief that human decisions are predominantly rational, research in neuroscience and psychology demonstrates that emotions play a dominant role. Renowned neuroscientist António Damásio introduced the concept of somatic markers, which are emotional responses linked to past experiences. These responses act as mental shortcuts, helping the brain prioritize certain options while discarding others.

For example, when deciding between two paths, an individual might unconsciously choose the one that evokes feelings of safety or comfort based on prior emotional experiences. Thus, emotions are not merely peripheral influences; they lie at the heart of decision-making.

How Emotions Influence Choices

Emotions not only guide choices but also shape how we perceive situations. Examples of how specific emotions impact the decision-making process include:

Fear: Can lead to defensive decisions, such as avoiding risks or seeking quick solutions to reduce anxiety.

Joy: Promotes optimism but can also result in overconfidence, leading to impulsive decisions.

Anger: Increases the propensity to take risks and may reduce the ability to consider long-term consequences.

Sadness: Often causes individuals to value emotional gains over material ones.

Recognizing these dynamics is essential to understanding not only your own decisions but also the motivations behind others' choices.

Controlling Emotions

Since emotions significantly influence decisions, learning to control them becomes an essential skill. Emotional control does not mean suppressing feelings but rather managing them so they serve your goals instead of dominating you.

Effective strategies include:

Recognizing Emotions: Identifying what you are feeling in the moment is the first step. Ask yourself, "Why am I feeling this?" and "How is this influencing my perception?"

Cognitive Restructuring: Replacing negative or irrational thoughts with more balanced interpretations. For example, transforming "I will fail" into "This is an opportunity to learn."

Mindfulness: Practicing mindfulness helps separate your emotions from the decision-making process, allowing you to act with greater clarity and control.

These practices not only strengthen your emotional intelligence but also enhance your resilience in challenging situations.

Manipulating Others' Emotions

Just as it is possible to manage your own emotions, it is also feasible to influence others' emotions. This is not limited to unethical manipulation but can be used to create harmony, build rapport, and facilitate communication.

Common techniques for influencing emotions include:

Priming Effect: Exposing someone to subtle stimuli that influence their emotions without their awareness. For instance, playing upbeat music before a negotiation can induce a sense of optimism.

Emotional Mirroring: Reflecting another person's emotions to create empathy and connection. If someone is anxious, showing slight concern can make them feel understood.

Emotive Storytelling: Sharing stories that evoke specific feelings, such as compassion or empathy, can shape how someone perceives a situation or decision.

For example, in a meeting where you need to convince a group to support an idea, telling a story that ties the proposal to the listeners' emotional values increases the likelihood of acceptance.

Collective Emotions and Group Decision-Making

In a group setting, emotions can amplify, creating phenomena such as emotional contagion. When one person expresses strong enthusiasm, for instance, it is common for others to match that energy. Similarly, the fear or anxiety of one member can spread, leading to decisions driven by panic or excessive caution.

To influence group decisions, consider:

Emotional Leadership: Projecting confidence and calm during tense moments can guide the group toward more rational decisions.

Creating an Emotional Climate: Adjusting the environment — lighting, music, language used — can shape the group's overall emotional state.

Conflict Management: Recognizing and validating everyone's emotions before seeking solutions fosters a sense of security and trust in the decision-making process.

Protecting Against Emotional Manipulation

If influencing emotions is a powerful skill, protecting yourself from emotional manipulation becomes equally vital. Recognizing when someone is attempting to manipulate your emotions allows you to maintain control over your choices.

Signs of emotional manipulation include:

Pressure to Respond Immediately: Creating urgency is a common tactic to discourage rational reflection.

Excessive Use of Guilt or Shame: These emotions are often exploited to coerce actions against your will.

Emotional Overreaction: Dramatic appeals to fear, joy, or sadness to distort your perception of a situation.

By identifying these tactics, you can slow down the process and evaluate the situation with a clearer and more objective perspective.

Ethical and Practical Applications

While emotional manipulation is often associated with unethical practices, it can also be used positively. For example, motivating a team by inspiring genuine enthusiasm about a project or encouraging a friend to overcome an emotional obstacle.

However, ethical use of this skill requires a careful balance between influencing for good and respecting others' emotional autonomy.

The Connection to Dark Psychology

Understanding emotions and their influence on decision-making is one of the pillars of dark psychology. It not only provides tools for understanding and influencing but also establishes a solid foundation for more advanced techniques of manipulation, persuasion, and narrative control.

By mastering this dynamic, you gain the ability not only to navigate the complex world of emotional interactions but also to shape them to your advantage. Every human choice lies at the intersection of reason and emotion — and those who understand this duality hold the power to guide the course of decisions.

Chapter 8
Introduction to Manipulation

Manipulation is an essential aspect of dark psychology, a concept that evokes both fascination and unease in equal measure. It refers to the ability to influence another person's thoughts, emotions, and behaviors—often subtly—to achieve a specific goal. However, manipulation is a double-edged sword: while it can be employed constructively and ethically, it can also cause significant harm when used selfishly or maliciously.

This chapter introduces the fundamentals of manipulation, its positive and negative applications, and its impact on both personal relationships and professional environments.

What Is Manipulation?

To manipulate is to exercise control or influence over someone in an indirect or disguised manner, often without the person realizing the true intent behind the actions. This practice can occur across various areas of life, from casual interactions to strategic negotiations, and its impact can range from insignificant to transformative.

Manipulation differs from persuasion. While persuasion respects autonomy and presents clear arguments to influence, manipulation operates in the shadows, concealing the manipulator's true intentions.

The Positive Aspects of Manipulation

Although often viewed negatively, manipulation can also be a force for good. When practiced ethically, it can motivate, protect, or facilitate important decisions.

Examples of positive manipulation include:

Encouraging someone: A teacher may use strategic praise to help a student overcome insecurities.

Protecting from dangers: A parent might selectively present information to steer a child away from a risky choice.

Facilitating change: A leader might manipulate group dynamics to build consensus around a beneficial decision.

In these cases, manipulation is employed with altruistic intentions, respecting the limits and well-being of those involved.

The Negative Aspects of Manipulation

Conversely, manipulation can be deeply harmful when used to deceive, exploit, or harm someone. This approach often results in emotional, psychological, or even financial damage.

Examples of negative manipulation include:

Emotional manipulation: Using guilt or shame to pressure someone into acting against their will.

Intentional deceit: Withholding critical information to gain an unfair advantage.

Exploitation of vulnerabilities: Identifying emotional or psychological weaknesses and using them for personal gain.

These tactics can undermine trust, destroy relationships, and leave lasting scars.

Elements of Manipulation

Regardless of intent, effective manipulation often follows a pattern that includes three main elements:

Control of Information: The manipulator selects, distorts, or omits information to shape the other person's perception.

Creation of Imbalance: Manipulation is most effective when the victim is in a vulnerable emotional or cognitive state, such as stress, fear, or uncertainty.

Concealment of Intentions: The manipulator avoids revealing their true motivations, presenting their actions as selfless or inevitable.

Recognizing these elements is crucial to protecting oneself from external manipulation and to using this skill ethically and effectively.

Common Manipulation Techniques

Manipulation takes many forms, ranging from subtle to overt. Some of the most common techniques include:

Gaslighting: Making someone question their own memory or perception, creating confusion and insecurity.

Information Isolation: Controlling access to information to limit the victim's ability to make independent judgments.

Excessive Praise: Using exaggerated compliments to build trust and pave the way for future requests.

Strategic Guilt: Inducing feelings of guilt to manipulate behaviors or decisions.

Commitment Escalation: Encouraging someone to continually invest in a decision or relationship, making it harder to back out even as the situation worsens.

When identified, these tactics can be neutralized through emotional resilience and rational analysis.

The Ethics of Manipulation

Manipulation is a powerful tool, and like any tool, its impact depends on how it is used. While some view it as inherently unethical, others argue that its morality depends on intent and context.

Manipulating someone to protect their well-being or prevent greater harm may be justified in certain circumstances. However, using manipulation to exploit or deliberately harm another person is widely considered unethical.

Self-awareness is critical to ensuring that the power of manipulation does not become a destructive force. Ask yourself: "Does my action respect this person's dignity and well-being?" If the answer is negative, it's time to reconsider your approach.

The Impact of Manipulation in Different Areas

Manipulation has practical implications across various areas of life:

Personal relationships: It can strengthen bonds when used to resolve conflicts or align goals but can also destroy trust when employed dishonestly.

Professional environments: Skilled manipulators may lead teams successfully but can also create toxic environments by exploiting colleagues or subordinates.

Negotiations: Manipulation can secure strategic advantages but, if discovered, may harm long-term relationships.

These examples demonstrate that the effects of manipulation extend beyond the immediate moment, influencing future perceptions and dynamics.

Protecting Yourself Against Manipulation

Understanding the fundamentals of manipulation is the first step to avoiding being victimized. Practical strategies include:

Recognize the Signs: Pay attention to behavioral changes, inconsistencies, or attempts to control information.

Strengthen Your Autonomy: Trust your own judgment and avoid making impulsive decisions.

Question Intentions: Analyze the motivations behind others' actions before reacting.

Set Boundaries: Do not hesitate to distance yourself from situations or individuals that repeatedly attempt to manipulate you.

These practices help build emotional resilience and ensure you maintain control over your choices.

The Connection to Dark Psychology

Manipulation is one of the most potent techniques within dark psychology. When understood deeply, it becomes a tool for influencing and protecting, depending on the context and intent. This chapter serves as an introduction to a complex and controversial territory that will be explored in greater detail in the following sections.

Manipulation is, at its core, the art of understanding and shaping human behavior. By mastering its principles, you gain not only significant power but also the responsibility to wield it wisely.

Chapter 9
Common Manipulation Techniques

When strategically employed, manipulation relies on techniques that exploit emotional, cognitive, and behavioral vulnerabilities. These strategies, though subtle, have the power to shape thoughts and actions without the target fully realizing their impact. This chapter demystifies the most common manipulation tactics, providing practical examples and methods to recognize, apply, or defend against them ethically.

The Essence of Manipulation Techniques

Manipulation techniques are not magic formulas; they work because they exploit natural patterns of human thought and behavior. The effectiveness of a technique lies in its application at the right moment, in the appropriate context, and with the proper level of subtlety.

When making decisions, people often seek mental shortcuts to save time and effort. These shortcuts, known as heuristics, provide fertile ground for manipulation techniques to thrive.

Emotion-Based Techniques

Emotions play a central role in manipulation, as they directly influence human decisions. Some of the most commonly used emotional tactics include:

Guilt

Guilt is one of the most powerful emotions for inducing submission. Manipulators often remind their victims of past mistakes or social obligations to create an exaggerated sense of responsibility.

Example: A coworker might say, "I always help you when you need it. Can't you help me now?"

Defense: Recognize the emotional appeal and evaluate whether the obligation is genuine or manipulative. Respond firmly, setting clear boundaries.

Excessive Praise

Excessive praise creates a false sense of trust and obligation. Feeling valued, the victim may become more likely to comply with subsequent requests.

Example: "You're so good at this; it would be amazing if you could handle this task for me."

Defense: Thank them for the compliment, but assess rationally whether the request makes sense. Do not feel pressured to accept just to meet expectations.

Fear Manipulation

Fear is used to create a sense of urgency and force impulsive decisions.

Example: A salesperson might say, "If you don't buy now, this exclusive offer will disappear."

Defense: Pause, take a deep breath, and logically evaluate whether the urgency is real or just a pressure tactic.

Cognitive and Behavioral Tactics

While emotions are a direct target, the logical mind can also be manipulated through cognitive biases and behavioral patterns. Some strategies include:

Reciprocity Bias

When someone does a favor or offers something, it creates an implicit obligation to reciprocate.

Example: A stranger offers a free sample and then suggests you buy a product.

Defense: Recognize the strategy and assess whether reciprocation is truly necessary or merely an artificial imposition.

Commitment Escalation

This technique involves small initial requests that lead to larger commitments.

Example: Someone asks you to "just attend a meeting" and eventually expects you to take on a more active role.

Defense: Before agreeing to the initial request, consider its long-term impact and establish clear boundaries from the start.

Scarcity Power

The perception that something is rare or limited increases its value and creates urgency.

Example: Promotions highlighting "Last units available" or "Only today."

Defense: Question the authenticity of the scarcity and make decisions based on your actual needs, not the pressure of the moment.

Social Manipulation

Beyond individual tactics, manipulators also exploit social dynamics to shape behaviors:

Group Pressure

Inducing conformity by emphasizing that the majority has already adopted an idea or behavior.

Example: "Everyone has already agreed to this. Why wouldn't you?"

Defense: Critically analyze the situation and trust your own values and judgments.

Isolation

Removing the victim from their support system to make them more vulnerable and dependent.

Example: A manipulator may suggest that friends or family are "toxic" to distance the target from external influences.

Defense: Maintain contact with trusted individuals and seek external perspectives on the situation.

Social Proof

Showing that others approve of or follow a particular action to influence someone's decision.

Example: "This product is the best seller in its category."

Defense: Question the relevance of social proof to your decision and evaluate whether it reflects your actual needs.

Recognizing Manipulation in Action

Early recognition is crucial to avoid falling victim to manipulation. Some warning signs include:

A sense of urgency or pressure to make a quick decision.

Feeling emotionally drained or confused after an interaction.

Behavioral changes that contradict your intentions or values.

Self-awareness and critical reflection help neutralize these effects.

The Ethics of Using Manipulation Techniques

While understanding these techniques provides power, ethical responsibility is non-negotiable. Using these strategies to assist or guide someone in a way that respects their autonomy is acceptable. However, exploiting them for selfish gain or to cause harm crosses moral boundaries.

Practical Applications and Protection

Manipulation techniques can be ethically used to:

Facilitate negotiations by creating harmony between parties.

Resolve conflicts by presenting alternatives that satisfy both sides.

Help someone overcome indecision by highlighting benefits or opportunities.

Similarly, protecting yourself requires practice and emotional resilience. Developing the ability to recognize and disarm these tactics is as important as learning to apply them.

Connection to Dark Psychology

Manipulation techniques are the beating heart of dark psychology. This chapter sheds light on the tools that transform theories into real-world practices, preparing the reader to explore more complex and advanced dynamics in human interactions.

Manipulation is not just an art; it is a science that demands study, observation, and reflection. When used wisely and ethically, it can become a powerful ally in the journey of influence and personal protection.

Chapter 10
The Psychology of Fear

Fear is one of the most primal and powerful human emotions, an evolutionary mechanism that ensures survival by alerting us to danger. However, fear can also be used as a tool of influence, capable of shaping decisions and behaviors in almost irresistible ways. This chapter delves into the psychological nature of fear, its impact on human behavior, and strategies to use it—or protect oneself from its power—within the context of dark psychology.

The Essence of Fear

Fear arises as a natural response to perceived threats, whether real or imagined. It is triggered by the activation of the limbic system in the brain, particularly the amygdala, which interprets danger signals and prepares the body to fight or flee. While essential for survival, fear is also an easily manipulable emotion, as it directly taps into basic instincts, often bypassing logical reasoning.

Manipulation through fear exploits this vulnerability. When someone is exposed to a threat, their focus narrows, reducing their ability to evaluate alternatives or resist influence.

Psychological Impacts of Fear

Fear triggers a series of emotional and behavioral responses that can be exploited to manipulate decisions:

Paralysis: In extreme fear, many people enter a state of inaction, becoming vulnerable to external guidance.

Obedience: Fear of punishment or social ostracism can lead to submission, even against one's will or values.

Search for Security: Frightened individuals tend to seek protection, making them more likely to accept solutions offering immediate comfort, even if detrimental in the long term.

These responses are widely used in political, social, and commercial contexts, where the creation of fear scenarios drives desired actions by manipulators.

Fear Manipulation Strategies

The tactics of fear manipulation vary in intensity and subtlety, but they all share the goal of inducing an emotional state conducive to influence.

Creating Threat Scenarios

One of the most common tactics is exaggerating or fabricating imminent dangers to force quick decisions.

Example: "If you don't act now, you'll lose everything you've built."

Effect: The victim feels urgency and loses the ability to calmly evaluate alternatives.

Using Authority

Messages from authoritative figures are perceived as more trustworthy, especially in fearful situations.

Example: A leader declares, "Only by following my instructions can we avoid this crisis."

Effect: Authority creates a sense of dependence and obedience.

Implied Threats

Instead of directly stating a danger, manipulators often subtly suggest risks to plant the seed of fear.

Example: "Do you really think you can trust people like that?"

Effect: Doubt and uncertainty trigger the fear of being deceived or betrayed.

The Ethical Use of Fear

While fear is often associated with negative manipulation, it can also be used ethically to motivate and protect. In contexts such as education or public health, fear can encourage positive behaviors.

Ethical Example: Highlighting the dangers of smoking in health campaigns to reduce tobacco use.

Practical Example: Warning coworkers about the risks of negligence in critical procedures.

The ethical use of fear respects individual autonomy by presenting clear and truthful information without malicious exploitation.

Strategies for Dealing with Fear

Managing fear—both one's own and that induced by others—is an essential skill in the arsenal of dark psychology. Strategies include:

Cognitive Restructuring

Question the validity of the threat. Ask yourself: "Is this situation as dangerous as it seems? What concrete evidence exists?"

Mindfulness

Practicing mindfulness helps regulate emotional responses to fear, enabling you to regain control over your reactions.

Knowledge Empowerment

Becoming informed about the topic or situation reduces vulnerability to unfounded or exaggerated threats.

These practices help maintain mental clarity, even in fear-inducing scenarios.

Recognizing Fear Manipulation

Signs of fear manipulation include:

Excessive Urgency: Pressure to make immediate decisions without time for reflection.

Vague Threats: Statements that create insecurity without providing specific details.

Appeals to Authority: Phrases like "Trust me, I know what's best."

Recognizing these signs allows you to disrupt manipulation before it takes hold.

Impacts of Fear in Different Contexts

Fear manipulation manifests in various domains:

Politics: Campaigns exploiting fear of the unknown, violence, or change to influence votes or control populations.

Marketing: Advertising that suggests the absence of a product will result in loss or discomfort.

Relationships: Using fear of abandonment or rejection to control partners or friends.

These examples demonstrate how fear can be used to influence or exploit, depending on the manipulator's intentions.

Protecting Yourself Against Fear Manipulation

Staying protected from fear manipulation requires practice and preparation. Effective measures include:

Self-Assessment: Reflect on your own fears and vulnerabilities, making them less susceptible to exploitation.

Reducing Urgency: Whenever you feel pressured to decide quickly, take a moment to consider your options.

Seeking Transparency: Demand concrete details and evidence before accepting alarming claims.

These practices strengthen your ability to resist manipulation, enabling more conscious and informed decisions.

The Connection to Dark Psychology

Fear is one of the most potent tools in dark psychology. It can be used to influence, protect, or even disarm manipulators. Understanding the psychology of fear is crucial to deciphering human motivations and developing effective strategies to shape behaviors or resist external pressures.

Mastering fear's impact on human interactions is not just about emotional survival; it is a step toward controlling your own reality and comprehending the complex world around you.

Chapter 11
Creating Rapport

Rapport is the foundation of every meaningful connection between individuals—a bridge of understanding and mutual trust that transcends words and formalities. It lies at the heart of successful social interactions, from casual conversations to critical negotiations. This chapter explores the art and science of building rapport, teaching you how to create genuine and effective connections capable of positively influencing those around you.

What is Rapport?

Rapport is the harmony or synchronicity that occurs when two or more people connect in a fluid and natural way. It is characterized by a sense of comfort, trust, and reciprocity that facilitates communication and understanding. When rapport is established, emotional barriers are reduced, and people become more receptive to new ideas and suggestions.

Although it may seem spontaneous, rapport is a skill that can be developed and improved with practice.

The Benefits of Rapport

Building rapport offers advantages in both personal relationships and professional settings. Notable benefits include:

Ease of Communication: Once trust is established, people feel more comfortable sharing information and thoughts.

Enhanced Influence: With rapport, you become a more persuasive figure, as people are inclined to listen to and consider the opinions of those they trust.

Conflict Resolution: Genuine connections help defuse tensions and find common solutions in challenging situations.

Strengthening Relationships: Rapport creates a solid foundation for lasting and mutually beneficial connections.

Key Elements of Rapport

To establish rapport effectively, it is essential to master three core elements:

Trust: Trust is the cornerstone of rapport. Building it requires authenticity, respecting others' boundaries, and demonstrating empathy.

Reciprocity: Rapport is a two-way street. Showing genuine interest and a willingness to listen and share in balance fosters a cycle of reciprocity.

Mirroring: Subtly imitating the body language, tone of voice, or word choices of the other person helps create a sense of familiarity and comfort.

Techniques for Building Rapport

Building rapport takes practice and attention to detail. Below are practical techniques to cultivate this skill:

Active Listening

Active listening involves giving your full attention to what the other person is saying, showing interest through facial expressions, nodding, and comments that validate their speech.

Example: Repeat or paraphrase a key point they've made, such as: "So, what you're saying is that flexibility is important to you, right?"

Identifying Commonalities

Finding shared interests, experiences, or values provides a common ground for connection.

Example: "I love traveling too! What's the most interesting destination you've visited?"

Adapting to Communication Style

Adjusting your speaking pace, volume, or word choice to match the other person's style can create a comfortable and cohesive atmosphere.

Example: If the person speaks slowly, match their pace to avoid seeming rushed or out of sync.

Authenticity

Forcing a connection or acting unnaturally can backfire. Be genuine and transparent in your intentions.

Rapport in Different Contexts

Rapport is a versatile skill that can be applied in various situations:

Personal Interactions

Building rapport in close relationships strengthens bonds and increases emotional intimacy. Showing empathy and genuine interest is particularly valuable in difficult conversations.

Professional Environments

In the workplace, rapport facilitates collaborations and negotiations. Demonstrating respect and finding mutual interests are effective strategies for creating productive connections.

Interactions with Strangers

In social gatherings or networking events, quickly building rapport can open doors to new opportunities. A warm smile and open-ended questions are good ways to start.

Exercises for Developing Rapport

Practicing rapport requires effort and repetition. Try the following exercises to strengthen this skill:

Mirroring Practice

During daily interactions, subtly mirror the posture or tone of voice of the other person. Observe how it impacts the dynamics of the conversation.

Asking Open-Ended Questions

Instead of questions that can be answered with "yes" or "no," use questions that encourage the other person to express themselves:

"What do you think about this?"

"Can you tell me more about how you came to that conclusion?"

Post-Conversation Analysis

After a conversation, reflect on what worked and what could have been improved in building rapport. Identify patterns and adjust your approach as needed.

Common Mistakes in Building Rapport

Despite being a powerful skill, rapport can be undermined by common mistakes:

False Empathy: Demonstrating superficial or exaggerated interest is easily noticed and can create distrust.

Frequent Interruptions: Interrupting the speaker shows a lack of respect and harms the connection.

Forcing Commonalities: Attempting to create similarities that don't exist can come across as artificial and uncomfortable.

Avoiding these mistakes helps establish authentic and effective connections.

Protecting Yourself from False Rapport

Rapport can also be used as a manipulation tool, where the connection is created solely to exploit or deceive. Signs of false rapport include:

Excessive and unfounded compliments.

Abrupt changes in tone or behavior after the initial connection.

A focus solely on gaining something from you rather than building a mutual relationship.

Staying vigilant and trusting your intuition can help you avoid falling into traps.

The Connection to Dark Psychology

Rapport is a cornerstone of dark psychology. It not only allows for the creation of trust and harmony but also lays the groundwork for more advanced techniques of influence and manipulation. When used ethically, rapport fosters positive and genuine interactions. However, in the hands of ill-intentioned individuals, it can become a tool for exploitation.

Building rapport is more than a social skill; it is a means of understanding and shaping human behavior. When mastered, it transforms every interaction into an opportunity for meaningful connection and positive impact.

Chapter 12
Mirroring Techniques

Mirroring is one of the most effective techniques for creating empathy and connection in human interactions. It is based on the psychological principle that people tend to feel more comfortable with individuals who demonstrate similarities to them. By discreetly replicating aspects of body language, tone of voice, communication style, or even speech rhythm, mirroring creates a sense of familiarity and trust. This chapter explores the science behind mirroring, its practical applications, and exercises to master this skill.

What Is Mirroring?

Mirroring is the act of subtly reflecting another person's behaviors, gestures, expressions, or communication patterns. It occurs naturally in positive interactions but can also be deliberately practiced to build rapport, persuade, or influence.

Psychologically, mirroring activates mirror neurons—brain structures that help people recognize and connect with the emotions and intentions of others. When someone perceives their behavior being reflected, even unconsciously, they are more likely to feel understood and at ease.

Why Does Mirroring Work?

Mirroring works because it promotes three main effects:

Creation of Empathy

By reflecting someone's behavior, you communicate that you are attuned to their emotions and intentions, fostering mutual empathy.

Reduction of Psychological Barriers

Mirroring reduces the perception of differences between you and the other person, facilitating communication and understanding.

Increased Receptivity

When someone perceives similarities in another person, they are more likely to trust and be influenced by them.

Elements of Mirroring

Mirroring can be applied to various aspects of interaction, from nonverbal cues to speech patterns.

Body Language

Mirror postures, gestures, or movements. For example, if the other person crosses their arms or leans forward, you can discreetly adopt the same position.

Facial Expressions

Reflect emotional expressions, such as smiling when the other person smiles or showing concern when they appear serious.

Tone of Voice and Speech Rhythm

Adjust your volume, tone, and speech speed to match the interlocutor's style. For instance, if someone speaks slowly and calmly, imitate that rhythm to create a comfortable environment.

Choice of Words

Use similar terms and phrases to reinforce the connection. If someone frequently says, "I feel that...," incorporate similar expressions into your speech.

Practical Exercises to Improve Mirroring

Mirroring, like any skill, improves with practice. Below are exercises to help develop and refine this technique:

Observation of Natural Interactions

In social situations, observe how people with good connections naturally mirror each other. Identify patterns and try to replicate them in your interactions.

Practice in Casual Conversations

During casual conversations, practice mirroring body language or tone of voice, starting with subtle reflections and gradually increasing precision.

Simulations in Front of a Mirror

Record yourself replicating different postures, gestures, and tones of voice. Review the recordings to assess whether your actions appear natural and congruent.

Feedback from Friends or Colleagues

Ask friends or colleagues to observe your interactions and provide feedback on your ability to mirror effectively.

Cautions When Practicing Mirroring

While mirroring is a powerful technique, it can become counterproductive if misused. Some pitfalls to avoid include:

Excessive Mirroring

Overdoing it by reflecting every movement or gesture may seem forced or intentionally imitative, causing discomfort.

Lack of Subtlety

Mirroring should be subtle and almost imperceptible. Obvious movements may be interpreted as disrespectful or manipulative.

Inappropriateness to the Context

Ensure that the mirrored behavior is appropriate for the situation. For example, adopting a casual posture in a formal environment may harm your credibility.

Applications of Mirroring

Mirroring can be used in a variety of contexts to facilitate connections and influence effectively:

Negotiations

Mirroring the other person's behavior during negotiations helps build rapport and facilitates favorable agreements.

Job Interviews

Discreetly reflecting the interviewer's posture and tone can create a sense of familiarity and increase your chances of making a positive impression.

Personal Relationships

Mirroring can strengthen bonds by demonstrating genuine empathy and understanding during intimate conversations or discussions.

Limitations and Ethical Considerations

As with all techniques of dark psychology, mirroring must be applied responsibly. It should not be used to manipulate or exploit others unethically. Instead, its practice should aim to foster clearer communication and genuine connections.

How to Recognize When You Are Being Mirrored

While mirroring is most effective when subtle, it is possible to identify when someone is attempting to use it:

Notice if the other person's gestures or postures immediately reflect your own.

Observe changes in their tone of voice or vocabulary that seem to align with your style.

Evaluate whether their actions feel natural or calculated.

Recognizing these practices can help you maintain control in interactions and avoid unwanted manipulation.

The Connection with Dark Psychology

Mirroring is a central tool in dark psychology, as it lays the foundation for more advanced influence techniques. It combines the power of empathy with the precision of observation, enabling you to shape behaviors and build solid relationships subtly.

When mastered, mirroring transforms ordinary interactions into opportunities for deep connection and impact. It is not merely a technique of influence but a skill that enriches how you relate to the world around you.

Chapter 13
Beliefs and Convictions

Beliefs are the invisible foundations that shape how we perceive the world and make decisions. They influence our actions, determine our values, and define the course of our lives. In this chapter, we explore the power of beliefs and convictions, how they can be shaped or transformed, and how understanding these principles can be used to influence, persuade, or protect oneself against manipulation.

What Are Beliefs and Convictions?

Beliefs are ideas or perceptions that a person accepts as true, while convictions are deeply rooted and emotionally charged beliefs that guide decisions and behaviors. These psychological structures form the core of our identity and serve as filters through which we interpret the world.

For example, someone who firmly believes in justice as a central value will likely make decisions that reinforce this view, rejecting actions perceived as unjust. Convictions, when reinforced by emotional experiences, become even harder to change, though not impossible to influence.

How Beliefs Are Formed

Beliefs do not arise out of nowhere; they are built over time and influenced by:

Personal Experiences: Direct experiences shape beliefs about what is safe, reliable, or meaningful.

Education and Culture: Cultural and educational environments establish norms and values that are often internalized as unconscious beliefs.

Social Influences: Friends, family, and authority figures play a crucial role in shaping beliefs.

Emotions and Rewards: Beliefs associated with positive emotions or rewards are more likely to take root.

A classic example is social conditioning: if a child is praised for demonstrating altruism, they may develop the belief that helping others is essential for gaining approval and respect.

The Role of Beliefs in Behavior

Beliefs act as silent guides, influencing decisions and behaviors without a person realizing it. They:

Define Priorities

Beliefs determine what a person values, shaping how they invest their time and energy.

Affect Judgments

Our beliefs serve as mental shortcuts to interpret information and make quick decisions.

Create Resistance

Deeply rooted beliefs can generate resistance to ideas or changes that contradict them, making it difficult to accept new concepts.

Transforming Beliefs Ethically

Influencing or transforming beliefs is a delicate process that requires empathy and respect. Ethical techniques for this transformation include:

Gradual Introduction of New Ideas

Introduce concepts subtly and progressively, allowing the person to explore them at their own pace.

Example: Instead of directly confronting a belief about healthy eating, share information and positive examples that spark curiosity.

Connecting with Past Experiences

Relate new ideas to the person's previous experiences, helping them find consistency between old and new beliefs.

Using Powerful Narratives

Telling compelling stories that exemplify the benefits of a new belief can be more effective than logical arguments.

These approaches respect the individual's autonomy and promote sustainable changes.

Strategically Influencing Beliefs

While belief transformation is often associated with personal growth, it can also be used strategically to influence decisions in negotiations, sales, or social dynamics. Some techniques include:

Creating Consistency

Encouraging someone to take small actions aligned with a new belief can reinforce the idea over time.

Example: Asking a colleague to take on a small role in an environmental project might lead them to adopt sustainability as a core value.

Appealing to Emotions

Beliefs are deeply connected to emotions. Genuine emotional appeals can be used to promote new perspectives.

Example: Showing the positive impact of a decision on others can motivate someone to reconsider selfish beliefs.

Using Models or Examples

Presenting behavioral models that embody the desired beliefs helps normalize and reinforce these ideas.

Recognizing Belief Manipulation

While influencing beliefs can be beneficial, it's essential to recognize when manipulation is being used unethically. Signs of manipulation include:

Excessive Pressure: Forcing someone to adopt a belief without allowing time for reflection or questioning.

Use of Fear or Guilt: Inducing negative emotions to manipulate behaviors and values.

Informational Isolation: Restricting access to alternative information to reinforce a specific belief.

Protecting oneself against these tactics requires a critical approach, consistently questioning the intentions behind external influences.

Practical Exercises for Shaping and Reinforcing Beliefs

To influence or transform beliefs ethically and effectively, practice the following exercises:

Identify Existing Beliefs: List someone's beliefs (or your own) and analyze their origin and impact. This will help you understand how to approach them effectively.

Build Bridges of Consistency: Find common ground between old beliefs and the new ideas you want to introduce. Use these points as bridges for change.

Present Positive Evidence: Reinforce new beliefs with practical examples and tangible benefits that encourage the adoption of new thought patterns.

The Importance of Ethics in Influencing Beliefs

Manipulating beliefs unethically can cause profound harm, eroding trust and damaging relationships. An ethical approach respects the person's autonomy and well-being, using influence as a tool to promote growth and learning.

The Connection with Dark Psychology

Beliefs are primary targets in dark psychology, as they shape not only behavior but also the perception of reality. Understanding how they work and how to influence them is essential for any strategy of persuasion or manipulation.

This chapter provides a solid foundation for exploring more advanced techniques that build on the power of beliefs and convictions, enabling you to skillfully navigate the complex world of human interactions. Transforming beliefs is not just an art; it is also a science that, when applied responsibly, can be a powerful force for positive change.

Chapter 14
Identifying Weaknesses

Identifying weaknesses is a crucial skill in dark psychology, as it enables you to understand the emotional, psychological, and behavioral vulnerabilities of an individual. This practice can be used to shape interactions, influence decisions, and even protect yourself from external manipulation. However, identifying weaknesses requires sensitivity and an ethical commitment to ensure its use respects the dignity and boundaries of others.

This chapter explores how to recognize and interpret weaknesses in others, the tools required for such analysis, and the ethical implications of applying this knowledge in personal and professional interactions.

What Are Weaknesses?

Weaknesses are emotional, psychological, or behavioral aspects that make a person more susceptible to influence or manipulation. They are not inherent flaws but human traits that can be exploited by those with knowledge and intent.

Common types of weaknesses include:

Fears: Specific phobias or concerns that create uncertainty.

Deep Desires: Intense aspirations or ambitions that may cloud judgment.

Emotional Deficiencies: Unmet needs, such as approval or affection.

Cognitive Blind Spots: Biases or beliefs that prevent someone from recognizing flaws in their reasoning.

Why Identify Weaknesses?

Understanding a person's weaknesses allows for more effective interactions by helping predict behaviors and shaping influence strategies. This can be useful in various contexts:

Negotiations: Exploring hidden motivations can facilitate agreements.

Conflict Resolution: Addressing someone's fears or needs can disarm resistance and promote cooperation.

Self-Protection: Recognizing your own weaknesses helps you avoid external manipulation.

Techniques for Identifying Weaknesses

Identifying weaknesses requires attention to detail and an analytical approach. Some of the most effective techniques include:

Careful Observation

Paying attention to behavior, body language, and tone of voice can reveal signs of vulnerability. For example:

Avoidance of certain topics may indicate hidden fears or insecurities.

Defensive postures, such as crossed arms or lack of eye contact, signal discomfort.

Analyzing Communication Patterns

How people talk about themselves, their problems, and their aspirations can expose their weaknesses.

Example: Someone who constantly seeks validation may have an emotional deficiency.

Using Open-Ended Questions

Asking open-ended questions encourages individuals to reveal valuable information.

Example: "What is most important to you in a difficult situation?"

Testing Reactions

Introducing hypothetical scenarios or sensitive topics can elicit emotional responses.

Example: Mentioning challenges related to a delicate theme and observing how the person reacts.

Identifying Contradictions

Inconsistencies between words and actions can hint at vulnerabilities.

Example: Someone who insists on being self-sufficient but frequently seeks support may be hiding insecurities.

Common Weaknesses Across Contexts

Weaknesses vary based on context and personality, but some are particularly common:

Fear of Rejection: The need for acceptance may lead someone to succumb to social or emotional pressures.

Need for Control: Individuals obsessed with control can be destabilized by uncertainties or unpredictable situations.

Exaggerated Ego: Overconfident people may be exploited through flattery or challenges.

Emotional Loneliness: The search for affection or attention often results in impulsive decisions to fill this void.

Strategies to Protect Yourself from Your Own Weaknesses

Just as you can identify others' weaknesses, it is crucial to recognize and address your own. Some strategies include:

Self-Awareness

Create a list of your fears, desires, and behavioral patterns that could be used against you. Recognizing these weaknesses is the first step to mitigating them.

Emotional Control

Learn to manage your emotions under pressure to avoid impulsive or manipulable decisions.

Critical Analysis

Regularly question your own motivations and perceptions, challenging beliefs that might make you vulnerable.

Strengthening Support Networks

Healthy, trusting relationships help balance emotional deficiencies and reduce susceptibility to manipulation.

The Ethics of Exploiting Weaknesses

Using knowledge of weaknesses unethically can result in significant emotional and psychological harm. Ethical application of this skill should focus on creating genuine connections, resolving conflicts, or helping others overcome obstacles rather than exploiting them for personal gain.

For example:

Ethical Use: Identifying a colleague's fear of failure and supporting them to overcome this insecurity.

Unethical Use: Exaggerating the risks of a situation to induce fear and gain an advantage in negotiation.

Exercises to Develop the Skill of Identifying Weaknesses

Observation Journal

Record daily interactions, highlighting behavioral or linguistic patterns that may reveal vulnerabilities.

Case Study Analysis

Analyze films or books with complex characters, identifying their weaknesses and how these are exploited or overcome.

Social Simulations

Practice using open-ended questions in casual conversations and observe how people respond emotionally.

Recognizing Attempts to Exploit Your Weaknesses

Protecting yourself from manipulation begins by identifying signs that someone is trying to exploit your weaknesses. These signs include:

Excessive Focus on Certain Topics: When someone repeatedly brings up areas where you feel insecure.

Induced Emotional Changes: If conversations often provoke intense or destabilizing emotions, manipulation may be at play.

Abrupt Behavioral Changes: Manipulative individuals often adjust their behavior based on your reactions.

The Connection to Dark Psychology

Identifying weaknesses is a core skill in dark psychology, as it allows you to understand the deeper motivations of those around you. When used responsibly, this skill can strengthen relationships, resolve conflicts, and even protect against negative influences.

Mastering the art of identifying weaknesses is not just a tool of influence; it is a path to understanding human complexity and shaping interactions with greater precision and impact. When practiced with empathy and ethics, this skill can transform both your life and the lives of those around you.

Chapter 15
The Psychology of Authority

The psychology of authority examines how people tend to obey or respond to figures of power or influence, often without questioning their intentions or legitimacy. This dynamic, deeply rooted in human behavior, can be a powerful tool for shaping actions and decisions, both constructively and manipulatively. In this chapter, we delve into the principles of authority, the factors that make it effective, and how to use it for positive influence, always within an ethical framework.

What Is Authority?

Authority is a form of social power that compels people to act or think in a certain way based on their perception of the legitimacy, knowledge, or control of a person or institution. This perception is not solely dependent on hierarchical position but also on subtle cues such as confidence, posture, and mastery of the subject matter.

Obedience to authority is a universal behavior with evolutionary roots. From humanity's earliest days, following leaders was essential for group survival. Today, while contexts have changed, the impulse to obey remains deeply ingrained.

The Principles of Authority

Robert Cialdini, in his work on persuasion, identified authority as one of the six fundamental principles of influence. Below are the elements that make authority effective:

Credibility: Trust in someone's knowledge or skills increases the likelihood of following their guidance.

Legitimacy: The perception that the authority has the right or power to command reinforces obedience.

Social Recognition: People recognized by others as authority figures tend to wield greater influence.

Visual Signals of Power: Uniforms, titles, posture, and even the environment where authority operates contribute to the perception of legitimacy.

The Impact of Authority on Behavior

The influence of authority on human behavior is profound and often subconscious. Stanley Milgram's famous obedience experiment demonstrated that ordinary individuals could commit acts against their personal values if instructed by an authority figure.

This impact is evident in various contexts:

Work Environments: Employees often follow instructions from superiors without question, even when they disagree.

Social Interactions: People tend to accept advice or suggestions from individuals they perceive as experts.

Marketing and Advertising: Celebrities or specialists promoting products create trust based on perceived authority.

How to Use Authority for Positive Influence

Authority, when wielded responsibly, can be a powerful tool for motivating, leading, and persuading. Here are strategies to apply it effectively:

Demonstrate Competence

People follow leaders who appear knowledgeable. Show solid expertise and confidence in your decisions.

Example: Before proposing an idea, present supporting data or examples.

Establish Legitimacy

Ensure your position as an authority is perceived as fair and relevant to the context.

Example: In a debate, emphasize your qualifications or experience related to the topic.

Project Confidence

Tone of voice, posture, and body language should convey assurance.

Example: Avoid hesitations or insecure gestures when speaking publicly.

Leverage Visual Signals of Authority

Use symbols that reinforce your position, such as appropriate attire, organized environments, or references to titles and roles.

Strategies to Naturally Reinforce Authority

Authority cannot be forced; it must be earned and recognized. To achieve this:

Be a Role Model: Actions speak louder than words. Demonstrate integrity and consistency in your decisions.

Develop Charisma: Charismatic authority is often more effective than imposed authority. Build emotional connections and inspire trust.

Create Alliances: Gain the respect of other leaders or influencers to strengthen your position of authority.

Manipulation Through Authority: Recognizing the Dangers

While authority is powerful, its unethical use can lead to abuse and manipulation. Common manipulative tactics based on authority include:

Fear Appeal: Exaggerating consequences of disobedience to induce submission.

Example: "If you don't follow this plan, you're putting everything at risk."

Title Appeal: Using titles or roles to avoid scrutiny, even when instructions are questionable.

Example: "I'm the expert here; you should listen to me."

False Authority: Creating the illusion of authority by adopting external signals of power without actual knowledge or legitimacy.

Example: Someone without relevant expertise using technical jargon to impress others.

Protecting Yourself Against Manipulative Authority

To avoid falling into traps of manipulative authority, practice the following:

Question Credentials: Verify whether the authority figure truly has the knowledge and legitimacy they claim.

Analyze Intentions: Ask yourself whether the advice or instructions serve a legitimate purpose or merely benefit the leader.

Strengthen Your Autonomy: Cultivate confidence in your own judgment and values, balancing obedience with critical reflection.

Exercises to Develop Your Own Authority

Practice Power Postures: Stand in front of a mirror and practice postures that convey confidence, such as keeping shoulders back and chin up.

Build Credibility Gradually: Share insights or information in small steps, earning trust through consistency and accuracy.

Master Active Listening: Demonstrating that you understand others' needs and concerns enhances your legitimacy as a leader.

The Connection to Dark Psychology

Authority is one of the pillars of dark psychology, as it taps into one of the most natural dynamics of human behavior: obedience. When used ethically, it can inspire trust and motivate positive actions. When manipulated, it becomes a dangerous tool that can compromise values and harm individuals.

Mastering the psychology of authority means understanding how to balance power with empathy. It involves leading without imposing, inspiring without intimidating, and influencing without exploiting. This skill is fundamental for successfully navigating the complex webs of human interaction and influence.

Chapter 16
Negotiation Techniques

Negotiating is one of the most valuable and universal skills in life. Whether closing a business deal, resolving a conflict, or simply deciding on the next family vacation destination, negotiation plays a role in nearly every human interaction. Within dark psychology, negotiation takes on a new dimension, incorporating techniques that leverage human behavior to maximize outcomes. This chapter unveils psychological strategies for effective negotiations, emphasizing the importance of preparation, observation, and persuasion.

The Essence of Negotiation

Negotiation is the process of reaching an agreement that satisfies the interests of all parties involved. However, effective negotiation goes beyond finding a middle ground; it involves understanding the other party's motivations, influencing their decisions, and shaping the final outcome in your favor.

Dark psychology comes into play as a tool to anticipate reactions, recognize weaknesses, and leverage emotional or cognitive dynamics to achieve favorable results.

The Pillars of Successful Negotiation

Before exploring advanced techniques, it's essential to understand the three basic pillars of any negotiation:

Preparation

Know your own goals, the limits of what you're willing to accept, and the interests of the other party. The more information you have, the more power you hold in the negotiation.

Communication

How you present your arguments is as important as their content. Use clear, persuasive language tailored to the context.

Strategic Flexibility

Be prepared to adjust your approach as the negotiation unfolds. A rigid negotiator misses opportunities.

Psychological Techniques in Negotiation

Incorporating principles of dark psychology can give you a significant advantage in any negotiation. The following techniques are particularly effective:

Anchoring

Start the negotiation by presenting an initial proposal that favors your interests. This starting point creates a psychological bias, influencing perceptions of what is reasonable for both parties.

Example: In a salary negotiation, an employer might offer a slightly lower figure, expecting the employee to adjust their expectations within that range.

Creating Scarcity

Use the perception of urgency to pressure the other party into making quick decisions.

Example: "This offer is only available until the end of the day."

Mirroring

Reflecting the other party's body language or communication style creates a subconscious connection, making them more receptive to your proposals.

Offering Alternatives

Present multiple options, all favorable to you. This creates the illusion of choice while maintaining control over the agreement's direction.

Example: "We can deliver the project in 15 days for an additional cost or in 30 days at no extra charge."

Structured Questions

Ask open-ended questions that guide the other party's thinking without appearing imposing.

Example: "What do you think would be fair in this situation?"

Reading Non-Verbal Cues

Pay attention to body language, tone of voice, and micro-expressions to assess the other party's sincerity or hesitation.

Managing Conflict in Negotiation

Negotiations often involve disagreements. Knowing how to handle conflicts is crucial to maintaining control and achieving the desired outcome.

Defuse Emotions

Acknowledge the other party's feelings and show empathy without compromising your position.

Example: "I understand this is important to you. Let's explore how we can resolve this together."

Reframe Arguments

If a proposal is rejected, reframe it to highlight the benefits differently.

Example: Instead of "This will cost you less," say, "This solution will allow you to save more in the long run."

Use the Power of Silence

After presenting a proposal, remain silent and let the other party reflect. The discomfort of silence can pressure them to respond or concede.

Advanced Influence Techniques in Negotiation

Role Reversal

Encourage the other party to imagine themselves in your position to foster empathy and justify your stance.

Example: "If you were managing this budget, what would you consider a viable solution?"

Conditional Offers

Link concessions to conditions that benefit you.

Example: "We can lower the price if you agree to a long-term contract."

Creating Gradual Commitment

Start with small requests that gradually lead to larger concessions.

Recognizing and Disarming Manipulative Tactics

Just as you can use psychological tactics, so can others. Recognizing them is essential to protecting your interests.

Extreme Demands

Outrageous initial requests are made to make smaller concessions seem reasonable.

How to respond: Ignore the extreme proposal and redirect focus to practical solutions.

Guilt or Emotional Pressure

Appeals to feelings can lead to unnecessary concessions.

How to respond: Stay rational and refocus on facts and figures.

False Urgency

Tight deadlines are used to force impulsive decisions.

How to respond: Question the validity of the deadline and request time to consider your options.

Exercises to Improve Negotiation Skills

Negotiation Simulations

Practice with friends or colleagues, experimenting with different techniques and strategies in fictional scenarios.

Post-Negotiation Analysis

After a negotiation, reflect on what worked, what didn't, and what could be improved.

Reading Non-Verbal Signals

In everyday interactions, practice identifying non-verbal cues, such as discomfort or hesitation, to enhance your perception.

Ethics in Negotiation

Using psychological techniques in negotiation must be balanced with ethical responsibility. Manipulating or deliberately deceiving the other party can undermine trust and harm future relationships. Instead, focus on creating mutual value and achieving solutions that benefit both parties.

The Connection with Dark Psychology

Negotiation is, at its core, a practical application of dark psychology. It involves understanding and influencing motivations, controlling emotional dynamics, and shaping decisions. When used skillfully and with integrity, knowledge of negotiation techniques can turn disputes into opportunities and foster stronger, more productive connections.

Mastering the art of negotiation is more than securing advantageous deals; it's about building relationships based on respect and positive influence, making you a reliable and effective negotiator in any context.

Chapter 17
The Power of Suggestion

Suggestion is a subtle yet incredibly powerful tool that acts directly on the subconscious, shaping perceptions, attitudes, and behaviors without the individual realizing the extent of its influence. When skillfully applied, suggestion can plant ideas, alter emotional states, and even lead to specific decisions in an almost imperceptible manner. This chapter delves into the fundamentals of suggestion, its practical applications, and strategies for its effective use, always keeping ethical boundaries in mind.

What is Suggestion?

Suggestion is the act of influencing someone's thoughts or behaviors through ideas or stimuli presented in an indirect or implicit way. Unlike a direct command, suggestion operates subtly, allowing the individual to feel as though their choices are entirely autonomous.

This technique is widely used in advertising, negotiations, leadership, and even personal relationships. It is effective because it exploits the workings of the subconscious, which processes information automatically and often without question.

Why Does Suggestion Work?

The power of suggestion is rooted in the functioning of the human brain. Several factors contribute to its effectiveness:

Subconscious Processing

The subconscious is highly receptive to subtle stimuli, especially when presented repetitively or with emotional significance.

Avoidance of Conscious Resistance

Since suggestion operates below the radar of the conscious mind, it bypasses the resistance that often accompanies direct approaches.

Trust in the Source

When the suggestion comes from someone perceived as trustworthy or authoritative, its effectiveness increases significantly.

Principles of Association

Suggestions often link ideas to positive emotions or desires, making them more appealing and harder to question.

Types of Suggestion

Suggestion can take various forms depending on the context and objective. Common types include:

Direct Suggestion

A clear and straightforward statement intended to influence.

Example: "You will feel more confident after practicing this technique."

Indirect Suggestion

Presenting an idea implicitly, allowing the person to reach the conclusion independently.

Example: "Many people find that small adjustments can make a big difference in their confidence."

Subliminal Suggestion

Discreet messages or stimuli that operate below the threshold of conscious perception.

Example: An image of a product associated with a scene of happiness in an advertisement.

Self-Suggestion

Influencing oneself through affirmations or repetitive practices, such as positive statements.

Example: "I am capable and resilient, and I can overcome this challenge."

How to Apply Suggestions Effectively

Effective application of suggestion requires subtlety and a clear understanding of the recipient's needs and motivations. Practical strategies include:

Create a Receptive Environment

A relaxed or emotionally positive setting makes the person more susceptible to suggestions.

Example: During a conversation, use a calm and friendly tone to create a sense of comfort.

Use Positive Language

Suggestions should emphasize what is desirable rather than focusing on what should be avoided.

Example: Replace "Don't make mistakes" with "Take care to ensure success."

Incorporate Repetition

Repeating an idea or phrase increases its subconscious acceptance.

Example: "You'll see how simple and effective this method is."

Ask Rhetorical Questions

Questions that don't require a direct answer prompt reflection and reinforce the suggestion.

Example: "Wouldn't it be amazing to achieve your goals faster?"

Use Stories or Metaphors

Narratives that exemplify the suggestion make it more engaging and memorable.

Example: "It's like planting a seed that, with care, grows and blossoms."

Suggestion in Different Contexts

Suggestion can be applied across various scenarios for specific purposes:

Advertising and Marketing

Companies use suggestion to associate products with positive emotions or desirable lifestyles.

Example: A commercial depicting happy people at a festive gathering while using a particular brand.

Negotiations

Indirect suggestions help shape the perception of a proposal's value or urgency.

Example: "Many of our partners are already benefiting from this exclusive deal."

Teaching and Leadership

Teachers and leaders can use suggestions to motivate or inspire confidence.

Example: "I'm confident you'll find a creative solution to this problem."

Personal Relationships

Suggestions help shape behaviors or attitudes without causing resistance.

Example: "You always seem so relaxed after a walk outdoors."

Protecting Against Unwanted Suggestions

While suggestion is a useful tool, it can also be employed manipulatively. Strategies to protect yourself include:

Critical Awareness

Stay mindful of how messages or stimuli influence your thoughts or emotions.

Constant Questioning

Evaluate the source and intent behind suggestions before accepting them.

Subconscious Strengthening

Practice positive self-suggestion to build barriers against external influences.

Exercises to Practice Suggestion

Experiment with Positive Phrasing

Practice transforming direct suggestions into positive affirmations and observe their impact.

Tell Stories

Use simple narratives in conversations to embed subtle suggestions, and observe the listener's response.

Daily Self-Suggestion

Create a list of positive affirmations and repeat them daily to reinforce desired habits or attitudes.

Ethics in the Use of Suggestion

Suggestion is powerful, but its use demands responsibility. Manipulating others for personal gain or exploiting vulnerabilities contradicts ethical principles and can cause emotional and relational harm. Instead, use suggestion to inspire, support, and foster positive connections.

The Connection with Dark Psychology

The power of suggestion lies at the heart of dark psychology, as it operates on the subconscious and subtly shapes behavior. Mastering this technique enables you to influence almost imperceptibly, creating opportunities to transform interactions and achieve goals strategically.

With practice and ethical intent, the use of suggestion becomes a tool to strengthen relationships, inspire change, and unlock the unlimited potential of human interactions.

Chapter 18
Conflict Management

Conflicts are an inevitable part of human interactions. Whether in professional settings, personal relationships, or broader social dynamics, disagreements can arise due to differences in interests, beliefs, or perspectives. However, conflicts also present opportunities to influence, shape behaviors, and even strengthen relationships—provided they are managed skillfully.

In this chapter, we explore conflict management techniques based on the principles of dark psychology. These strategies go beyond simply resolving disputes; they empower you to use conflicts as a tool to achieve objectives, strengthen your position, and create favorable solutions.

What is Conflict Management?

Conflict management is the process of addressing disagreements in a way that meets the interests of the involved parties, prevents unnecessary escalation, and seeks mutually beneficial outcomes. Within dark psychology, this skill takes on nuances that enable not only problem resolution but also the shaping of perceptions and power dynamics.

Fundamental Principles of Conflict Management

Before applying advanced techniques, it is essential to understand the principles that underpin effective conflict management:

Understanding Emotions

Conflicts are often fueled by intense emotions such as anger, fear, or frustration. Recognizing and validating these emotions helps defuse tensions.

Identifying Underlying Interests

Behind every position or explicit demand lie deeper interests and needs. Identifying these motivations allows for a more strategic approach to the conflict.

Maintaining Control

In conflict situations, staying calm and projecting confidence enhances your ability to influence and lead.

Psychological Techniques for Managing Conflicts

Dark psychology provides powerful tools to turn conflicts into opportunities for influence and resolution. Below are some of the most effective techniques:

Building Rapport in Tense Situations

Establishing a connection with the other party, even in the midst of conflict, reduces resistance and facilitates communication.

Example: Use mirroring to reflect the other person's tone of voice or posture, creating a sense of familiarity.

Disarming with Empathy

Demonstrating genuine understanding of the other person's emotions can deactivate defensive reactions.

Example: "I understand why you're frustrated. Let's work together to find a solution."

Reframing Perspectives

Present the conflict in a new light, highlighting potential benefits or solutions.

Example: "If we can resolve this, both of us will come out stronger."

Strategic Use of Silence

After making a statement or proposal, remain silent. This creates discomfort, which may lead the other party to yield or reconsider their position.

Guiding Questions

Open-ended or reflective questions steer the other person's thinking toward areas that favor your position.

Example: "What do you think would be needed to resolve this situation fairly?"

Handling Resistance

Resistance is a common reaction in conflicts, especially when parties feel their interests are threatened. Knowing how to address these barriers is crucial for progress.

Breaking Down Barriers

Identify the reasons behind the resistance and address them directly.

Example: "It seems you're concerned about the impact of this decision. Let's explore that together."

Positive Reinforcement

Emphasize the gains or advantages of yielding or cooperating.

Example: "If we take this approach, you can save time and resources."

Creating Small Commitments

Start with smaller concessions to create a sense of progress and pave the way for larger agreements.

Turning Conflicts into Opportunities

When well-managed, conflicts can become opportunities to strengthen relationships, establish authority, and even achieve previously unattainable goals.

Building Trust

Demonstrating skill in conflict resolution enhances your credibility and reliability.

Establishing Leadership

Taking control of challenging situations projects authority and competence.

Strengthening Relationships

Resolving conflicts collaboratively fosters a sense of partnership and mutual respect.

Practical Tools for Conflict Management

Conflict Map

Create a diagram that identifies the parties involved, their interests, and points of convergence. Use this as a guide to structure your approach.

Case Studies
Analyze past conflicts (yours or others') to identify patterns of behavior and effective strategies.

Simulations
Practice conflict management in fictional scenarios with colleagues or friends, applying techniques for emotional disarmament and negotiation.

Common Mistakes in Conflict Management
Even the most effective strategies can fail if certain errors are made:

Ignoring Emotions: Focusing solely on facts or logic can alienate the other party, who wants their emotions acknowledged.

Avoiding Conflict: Avoiding necessary discussions can exacerbate the problem and harm relationships.

Reacting Impulsively: Responding with anger or frustration undermines your credibility and makes resolution harder.

Avoiding these mistakes requires self-awareness and consistent practice.

Ethics in Conflict Management
Using dark psychology to resolve conflicts requires an ethical balance. Manipulating or exploiting the vulnerabilities of the other party may lead to immediate gains but will undermine trust and respect in the long term. An ethical approach involves:

Seeking solutions that benefit all parties whenever possible.

Avoiding dishonest manipulations or intimidation.

Respecting the dignity and boundaries of others.

The Connection to Dark Psychology
Conflict management is a direct application of the principles of dark psychology, combining observation, empathy, and strategic influence to shape human dynamics. When mastered, this skill transforms challenging situations into opportunities to reinforce your position, build relationships, and achieve favorable outcomes.

Conflicts are not obstacles; they are gateways to growth and transformation. With the right tools, every disagreement can become a chance to strengthen your emotional intelligence and shape interactions in a positive, impactful way.

Chapter 19
Group Behavior

Group behavior is a complex manifestation of human interactions, where individual actions and decisions are influenced—sometimes even determined—by collective dynamics. Understanding and applying the principles governing this behavior is a powerful skill, enabling you not only to predict group reactions but also to influence their direction.

In this chapter, we explore how dark psychology can be applied to understand and influence group dynamics, whether in social, professional, or leadership contexts.

What is Group Behavior?

Group behavior refers to how individuals act and react in a collective environment. It is guided by norms, social pressures, and emerging leadership, often shaping decisions and behaviors that differ from what individuals would do in isolation.

Among the most common phenomena in group behavior are:

Conformity: The tendency to align thoughts or actions with the majority.

Polarization: The intensification of opinions or attitudes when discussed in a group.

Groupthink: A pursuit of consensus that suppresses divergent ideas.

Deindividuation: Loss of personal identity in favor of the group identity.

Why Do People Behave Differently in Groups?

The shift in individual behavior within a group stems from profound psychological factors, including:

Social Pressure

The need for acceptance drives individuals to adjust their behavior to avoid conflict or rejection.

Diffusion of Responsibility

In a group, people feel less personal accountability, which can lead to actions they would not take alone.

Leadership Influence

Formal or informal leaders significantly shape the group's actions and beliefs.

Group Norms

Implicit or explicit expectations about how members should behave guide the direction of interactions.

Strategies to Understand Group Behavior

To influence a group, you must first understand it. The following strategies help decipher group dynamics:

Observe Roles and Hierarchies

Identify formal and informal leaders, as well as influential followers. These figures shape the group's direction.

Example: In a work team, those who frequently propose ideas or resolve conflicts tend to hold more influence.

Analyze Unwritten Norms

Pay attention to repeated behaviors and implicit expectations that maintain group cohesion.

Detect Subgroups

Larger groups often divide into smaller subgroups, each with its own interests and dynamics.

Identify Communication Patterns

Who speaks the most? Who is frequently ignored? These dynamics reveal levels of influence and power.

Psychological Techniques to Influence Groups

Dark psychology offers several techniques to shape and direct group behavior. Some of the most effective include:

Creating Alignment

Promote a sense of shared purpose to unite the group around an idea or goal.

Example: "We all want this project to succeed, and each of us plays a crucial role in making that happen."

Stimulating Conformity

Present ideas as the group norm or consensus.

Example: "Most of us agree this is the best approach. Let's move forward."

Reinforcing Leadership

Leverage your position as a formal or informal leader to guide the group, exuding confidence and assurance.

Example: "I trust everyone's potential here to overcome this challenge together."

Manipulating Social Pressure

Encourage adherence to norms by highlighting positive behaviors and isolating disruptive attitudes.

Example: "I admire how everyone is staying focused. Let's ensure we keep this momentum."

Exploiting Rivalries

If there are subgroups or rivalries, use them to foster healthy competition or to divide and conquer.

Handling Resistance in Groups

Not all group members will respond uniformly to your attempts at influence. Knowing how to address resistance is critical:

Active Listening

Acknowledge the concerns of resistant members, demonstrating that their opinions are valued.

Engage Influencers

Bring respected figures within the group to your side, increasing acceptance of your message.

Dissolve Resistance with Empathy

Reframe objections as opportunities to refine or improve ideas.

Example: "You've raised an important point. How can we integrate that into our plan?"

Turning Groups into Tools of Influence

Groups wield power not only within their internal dynamics but also in their external influence. Learn to harness this power to create broader impact:

Mobilizing Masses

Transform the group into a cohesive force that drives a cause or message.

Example: "If we all share this idea with our networks, we can make a significant impact."

Creating Examples

Use the group as a success story to demonstrate the strength of your ideas or leadership.

Cascading Influence

The impact of a group can extend beyond its immediate boundaries, shaping opinions and behaviors in other people or groups.

Common Mistakes When Working with Groups

Avoid pitfalls that can undermine your ability to influence or lead groups:

Ignoring Subgroups or Alliances: Overlooking internal dynamics can lead to unexpected divisions or resistance.

Excessive Imposition: Forcing conformity or leadership without building rapport may breed distrust or rebellion.

Lack of Clear Purpose: Groups without clear objectives or direction often become disorganized and ineffective.

Exercises to Develop Group Behavior Skills

Observing Real Groups

Attend meetings or group events and take note of dynamics such as leadership, conformity, and resistance.

Simulating Group Dynamics

Organize a small group to discuss a fictional topic and practice influencing the direction of the conversation.

Analyzing Case Studies

Study historical or modern examples of group behavior, identifying patterns and applying the concepts learned.

Ethics in Group Influence

Manipulating groups for personal gain or to harm others is an unethical use of dark psychology techniques. Ethical group influence should:

Promote clear and positive objectives.

Respect the autonomy of members.

Avoid excessive or dishonest pressures.

The Connection to Dark Psychology

Group behavior is one of the most fascinating fields in dark psychology. Its complexity offers countless opportunities for influence, from shaping collective decisions to creating larger, more impactful movements.

Mastering group dynamics is not just a tool for power; it is a way to better understand human behavior in its collective essence. When used skillfully and with integrity, knowledge of group interactions can transform you into a powerful and respected leader or influencer.

Chapter 20
Building Credibility

Credibility is the cornerstone of influence. Without it, even the best ideas can be ignored, and attempts at persuasion can fail. This chapter delves into the art of building and maintaining credibility, analyzing the factors that make it robust and strategies for applying it in different contexts. Within dark psychology, credibility is not just a perceived quality but also a tool intentionally shaped to gain social power and influence behavior.

What Is Credibility?

Credibility is the perception of trustworthiness, competence, and honesty that people have of you. It's not just about being honest or experienced but about appearing reliable and capable in the eyes of others. Credibility is a social construct shaped by behavior, communication, and reputation.

It is built upon three fundamental pillars:

Trust: People need to believe that you are sincere and have good intentions.

Competence: Demonstrating knowledge or skill in relevant areas is essential.

Consistency: Your actions must align with your words to sustain your credibility.

The Importance of Credibility in Influence

Credibility increases receptiveness and reduces resistance. In negotiations, leadership, or persuasion, being perceived as trustworthy and competent puts you at an advantage. Without credibility, any attempt to influence others will be met with suspicion or rejection.

For example, a respected leader can propose significant changes to a team, while someone with low credibility will face resistance, even if their ideas are superior.

How to Build Credibility

Building credibility is an ongoing process that requires consistency and attention to detail. Here are practical strategies to develop it:

Demonstrate Knowledge

Be prepared and well-informed about the topics at hand. Showcase expertise through relevant data, examples, and insights.

Example: "Recent studies show that implementing this strategy can increase efficiency by up to 30%."

Communicate Clearly

Clarity in communication conveys confidence and security. Use accessible language and avoid unnecessary jargon.

Example: Instead of using overly technical terms, explain complex concepts with simple analogies.

Keep Promises

Credibility depends on your ability to fulfill commitments, even in challenging situations.

Example: If you commit to delivering something by a specific date, prioritize meeting that deadline.

Be Transparent

Admitting faults or limitations demonstrates honesty and strengthens your position as a trustworthy figure.

Example: "I acknowledge I made a mistake on this point, but I have already taken steps to correct the situation."

Show Genuine Interest

Show empathy and concern for others' interests and well-being.

Example: "How can I help you overcome this obstacle?"

Nonverbal Elements of Credibility

Nonverbal communication plays a crucial role in how credibility is perceived. Even without words, posture and expressions can reinforce or undermine your image.

Posture and Gestures

Maintain an upright and open posture, avoiding nervous or excessive gestures. This conveys confidence and composure.

Eye Contact

Looking directly into people's eyes creates a sense of connection and sincerity.

Tone of Voice

A balanced and firm tone communicates authority without appearing arrogant.

Psychological Strategies to Enhance Credibility

Dark psychology offers insights into how to shape the perception of credibility strategically:

Associate with Authority Figures

Working with or being seen with respected individuals automatically boosts your credibility through association.

Example: Mentioning collaborations with experts or industry leaders.

Subtle Mirroring

Adjusting your body language or tone of voice to match the other person's creates a sense of empathy, reinforcing your trustworthiness.

Leverage Social Proof

Demonstrating that others trust or follow you strengthens your image.

Example: "Our most satisfied clients often mention how our solutions exceeded their expectations."

Maintaining Credibility

Building credibility is challenging, but maintaining it requires ongoing effort. Any inconsistency or negligent behavior can damage your reputation.

Consistency

Be coherent in your actions and communications. Small contradictions can cause disproportionate harm.

Accountability

Take responsibility for your mistakes, showing maturity and a commitment to improvement.

Continuous Improvement

Keep developing your skills and knowledge to sustain your position as a competent figure.

Recognizing Manipulations of Credibility

Not everyone who appears credible is genuine. Identifying manipulations is crucial to avoid being inappropriately influenced.

False Authority

Someone using titles or jargon without true knowledge to impress others.

Fabricated Social Proof

Testimonials or claims from dubious sources used to create an illusion of trust.

Avoiding Difficult Questions

When someone evades direct questions or refuses to provide clear information, it may indicate an attempt to mask incompetence.

Exercises to Develop Credibility

Regular Self-Review

Assess your consistency and promise-keeping weekly, identifying areas for improvement.

Communication Simulations

Practice important presentations or conversations with friends or colleagues to receive feedback on your posture, tone, and clarity.

Learning Journal

Keep a record of new skills or knowledge acquired, reinforcing your expertise base.

Ethics in Using Credibility

When manipulated to deceive or exploit, credibility can cause irreparable harm to others' trust. Use it to promote transparency, solve problems, and build positive relationships.

Connection to Dark Psychology

Credibility is one of the most powerful tools in dark psychology. When used strategically, it allows you to shape perceptions and open doors to influence and leadership. However, like any tool, its impact depends on the intent behind its use.

Building credibility is more than a strategy; it is a reflection of integrity, competence, and trust. When mastered, this skill transforms your ability to persuade, lead, and inspire in any context.

Chapter 21
Storytelling Techniques

Storytelling, or the art of telling stories, is a powerful skill that transcends cultures and eras. Compelling stories capture attention, evoke emotions, and shape perceptions in ways that few other methods can. In the context of dark psychology, storytelling is an essential tool for influencing people and effectively conveying ideas. This chapter explores the techniques that make a narrative impactful, detailing how to apply them to captivate attention, persuade, and influence decisions.

Why Is Storytelling So Effective?

Storytelling works because it appeals to both logic and emotions, creating an experience that deeply resonates with listeners. Some reasons for its effectiveness include:

Emotional Connection

Stories evoke empathy, allowing the listener to place themselves in the characters' shoes and engage emotionally.

Memorability

Information conveyed through a narrative is easier to remember than isolated data or arguments.

Subtle Persuasion

A well-told story can introduce ideas or values indirectly, reducing the audience's resistance.

Personal Identification

People tend to identify with characters or situations, adopting the story's lessons as part of their own beliefs.

Essential Elements of a Good Story

A powerful story is built on specific elements that capture attention and engage the audience:

Relatable Characters

Characters should be recognizable and evoke empathy. They don't need to be perfect but must have clear motivations and real challenges.

Conflict and Resolution

Every good story has a central conflict that creates tension and sustains interest, followed by a satisfying resolution.

Emotional Appeal

The story should touch the audience's emotions—whether by inspiring, surprising, or moving them.

Central Message

A good narrative conveys a clear idea or moral without needing to state it explicitly.

Techniques for Creating Engaging Stories

Effective storytelling requires practice and attention to detail. Here are specific techniques to enhance your narratives:

Start with a Hook

The beginning of the story should immediately grab attention. Use an intriguing question, an unexpected situation, or a curious detail.

Example: "Have you ever wondered how one seemingly insignificant decision can change your entire life?"

Set the Scene

Help the audience visualize the story by describing the setting and characters with enough detail to create a clear mental picture.

Build Tension Gradually

Introduce challenges or obstacles slowly, increasing intensity to maintain interest.

Incorporate Visual and Sensory Elements

Use descriptions that activate the senses, such as sounds, smells, or textures, to make the story more vivid.

Example: "The aroma of fresh coffee filled the air as he struggled to find the courage to speak the truth."

Include Surprises

Unexpected twists or revelations keep the audience engaged and curious about the outcome.

End with Impact

The conclusion should be memorable, leaving a lasting impression or a clear lesson.

Applications of Storytelling in Influence

Storytelling is a versatile tool that can be applied in various contexts to influence and persuade:

Marketing and Advertising

Brands use stories to create emotional connections with consumers, showcasing how their products or services solve real problems.

Example: A commercial showing a happy family after using a household product.

Negotiations

A story illustrating benefits or risks can shape the other party's perception and facilitate agreements.

Example: "I remember a client facing the same challenge as you. By adopting this solution, they achieved impressive results."

Leadership

Leaders inspire and motivate their teams by telling stories of overcoming obstacles, innovation, or collective purpose.

Education

Stories make complex concepts more accessible and memorable for students or learners.

Psychological Strategies in Storytelling

Incorporating principles of dark psychology into storytelling enhances its effectiveness in capturing and shaping perceptions:

Creating Identification

Structure your story so that the audience sees themselves in the characters or situations presented.

Planting Subtle Ideas

Introduce concepts or values indirectly, allowing the audience to adopt them as if they were their own.

Using Powerful Metaphors

Metaphors and analogies simplify complex ideas and create instant emotional connections.

Example: "Facing this challenge is like climbing a mountain; every step feels hard, but the view from the top is worth it."

Reinforcing Positive Emotions

Conclude your story with positive feelings to create a favorable association with your message.

Practical Exercises to Improve Storytelling

Write Short Stories

Create stories of up to 200 words with a clear beginning, middle, and end. Focus on conveying a central message.

Practice Oral Storytelling

Share stories in casual conversations, observing how different audiences react. Adjust details and tone as needed.

Analyze Successful Narratives

Study commercials, speeches, or books that use effective storytelling. Identify the elements that make these stories impactful.

Common Storytelling Mistakes

Avoid pitfalls that can weaken your narrative:

Excessive Details

Unnecessary information can bore the audience and dilute the central message.

Lack of Emotional Connection

A story that doesn't evoke emotions will have little impact, even if it is logical or informative.

Weak Ending

An unsatisfying conclusion can negate the impact of a good narrative.

Ethics in Storytelling

While storytelling is a powerful tool, using it to deceive or manipulate is unethical. Ensure that your stories are authentic and promote positive values.

Connection to Dark Psychology

Storytelling is a practical and powerful application of dark psychology principles. It combines emotional appeals, subtle logic, and structured narrative to influence thoughts and behaviors. When used skillfully and with integrity, it transforms interactions and fosters deep connections.

Mastering the art of storytelling is more than a communication skill; it is a way to capture the hearts and minds of people, shaping the world around you with creativity and purpose.

Chapter 22
Manipulating Perceptions

Perception is the lens through which people interpret the world around them. Altering this lens can influence how situations, people, and ideas are understood, consequently shaping decisions and behaviors. Manipulating perceptions is not just a tool of dark psychology but also an essential skill in leadership, negotiations, marketing, and interpersonal relationships. This chapter unveils the mechanisms of perception, techniques to shape it, and the ethical considerations required when utilizing it.

What Is Perception?

Perception is the psychological process through which people interpret sensory stimuli, forming a subjective understanding of reality. It is influenced by internal factors, such as beliefs, emotions, and past experiences, as well as external factors, such as context and the presentation of information.

Manipulating perception occurs when these factors are intentionally adjusted to influence how a person perceives a situation or idea.

How Can Perception Be Manipulated?

Manipulating perceptions requires a deep understanding of how the brain processes information. Some common methods include:

Context Control

The environment or framework in which a situation is presented directly affects how it is perceived.

Example: The same product appears more appealing when displayed in a luxury store than in a simple market.

Information Selection

Highlighting certain aspects while concealing others shapes the perception of what is important or relevant.

Example: In a negotiation, emphasizing the benefits of a proposal while minimizing its drawbacks.

Exploitation of Cognitive Biases

Leveraging mental shortcuts, such as confirmation bias, where people tend to accept information that reinforces their pre-existing beliefs.

Emotion Manipulation

Linking an idea or event to a strong emotion (positive or negative) alters how it is perceived.

Fundamental Principles for Manipulating Perceptions

Successful application of this skill requires attention to the following principles:

Create Positive Associations

Connect the idea or person to positive images, words, or events.

Example: Presenting a plan during a celebration or moment of success increases its acceptance.

Control the First Impression

A person's initial exposure to a situation significantly shapes their future perception.

Example: A leader exuding confidence and competence during the first interaction establishes a positive foundation for future relations.

Apply the Principle of Comparison

Present a less attractive alternative alongside the desired option to make it more favorable.

Example: In a pricing proposal, offer a more expensive plan before presenting the one you aim to sell.

Reinforce Perception Through Repetition

Ideas repeated consistently become more acceptable and familiar, gradually shaping perception.

Techniques for Manipulating Perceptions

The following techniques detail how to shape perceptions effectively:

Use of Persuasive Language

Choose words that create positive mental images or strategically guide thought.

Example: Replace "expenses" with "investment" when presenting a budget.

Creation of Narratives

Craft stories that shape the audience's perception of an idea or situation.

Example: When launching a product, tell the story of how it was developed to solve a specific problem.

Information Management

Present facts selectively, highlighting those that favor your position.

Example: In a performance report, emphasize positive outcomes and frame negative results as opportunities for improvement.

Exploitation of Visual Power

Use images, graphics, or even colors to reinforce the intended message.

Example: A professionally designed document with strategic colors conveys seriousness and credibility.

Timing Manipulation

The timing of information presentation can alter its perception.

Example: Releasing challenging news after a positive announcement minimizes the negative impact.

Practical Examples of Perception Manipulation

In Marketing

Presenting a product as "the best seller" creates a perception of popularity, even if the data pertains to a niche market.

In Leadership

Publicly recognizing small team successes shapes the perception of progress and collective competence.

In Interpersonal Relationships

When faced with criticism, reframe the situation to highlight your strengths or capacity for growth.

Protecting Yourself from Perception Manipulation

As it is crucial to know how to shape perceptions, it is equally essential to safeguard against external influences attempting to manipulate you.

Question the Context

Assess whether the environment or framing is disproportionately influencing your perception.

Seek Complete Information

Try to obtain different perspectives before forming an opinion.

Beware of Emotional Appeals

Identify whether emotions are being used to steer your interpretation.

Trust Intuition but Verify Facts

If something seems too good or too bad to be true, investigate further before accepting it.

Practical Exercises to Develop the Skill

Reframing

Choose an everyday situation and practice presenting it in different ways, highlighting positive or negative aspects.

Analyzing Advertisements

Review commercials to identify how perception is shaped through images, language, and context.

Creating Comparisons

Practice creating comparison scenarios to present an option as more advantageous.

Ethics in Manipulating Perceptions

Manipulating perceptions unethically, such as distorting information to deceive, can cause irreparable damage to trust and reputation. Use these techniques to promote transparency, foster harmony, and achieve positive objectives without compromising integrity.

The Connection to Dark Psychology

Perception manipulation is a core skill in dark psychology, allowing influence over how others view the world and make decisions. When used responsibly, this skill not only maximizes your impact in social and professional interactions but also enhances your ability to protect yourself from external influences.

Mastering the art of shaping perceptions involves understanding that reality is often not objective but a reflection of what people choose to see. When applied effectively, this skill transforms challenges into opportunities and ideas into concrete actions.

Chapter 23
Introduction to Gaslighting

Gaslighting is one of the most insidious techniques of psychological manipulation. It is a process that induces the victim to doubt their perception of reality, memories, and even their sanity. This chapter examines the concept, characteristics, and effects of gaslighting, emphasizing how to recognize it, protect yourself against it, and ethically use knowledge of this technique to strengthen psychological resilience.

What Is Gaslighting?

The term "gaslighting" originates from the play Gas Light (1938), in which a character manipulates his wife to the point where she believes she is losing her mind. In practice, gaslighting involves the continuous manipulation of information to make the victim question their perceptions, memories, or judgments.

This technique is often used in personal relationships, workplace power dynamics, and even political campaigns. Its primary goal is to undermine the victim's confidence in themselves, making them more vulnerable to the manipulator's influence.

Characteristics of Gaslighting

Understanding gaslighting requires recognizing its key characteristics:

Persistent Denial

The manipulator denies facts or events that the victim clearly remembers.

Example: "I never said that. You're making things up."

Invalidation of Feelings

The victim is led to believe their emotions or reactions are exaggerated or irrational.

Example: "You're being too sensitive. It's not that serious."

Distortion of Reality

The manipulator creates narratives that contradict the victim's perception, leaving them unsure of what is real.

Example: Altering details of an event to confuse the victim.

Psychological Isolation

The victim is discouraged from seeking external opinions, increasing their dependency on the manipulator.

Example: "No one will believe you. Only I understand what's going on."

How Gaslighting Works

Gaslighting operates through a combination of psychological factors that affect the victim's mind:

Repetition: The manipulator consistently denies reality or presents a distorted version until the victim begins to question their own perception.

Confusion: The victim is bombarded with contradictory information, weakening their judgment.

Dependence: The manipulator positions themselves as the only reliable source of truth or stability.

Effects of Gaslighting

The effects of gaslighting can be devastating to the victim's emotional and psychological health, including:

Loss of Self-Confidence: The victim begins to doubt their reasoning and memory.

Social Isolation: Feeling misunderstood, the victim may withdraw from friends and family.

Anxiety and Depression: Constant emotional manipulation can lead to chronic mental distress.

Dependence on the Manipulator: The victim increasingly relies on the manipulator for guidance, perpetuating the cycle of abuse.

How to Recognize Gaslighting

Identifying gaslighting is the first step to combating it. Look for these warning signs:

You frequently question your memory or perception, even in clear situations.

You feel confused or unable to make decisions without validating them with someone else.

You receive constant feedback that you're being exaggerated or irrational.

You notice a disconnect between your experience and the narrative presented by someone else.

Strategies to Combat Gaslighting

If you suspect you are a victim of gaslighting, the following strategies may help:

Trust Your Perceptions: Keep a journal to record events and feelings. This will help reaffirm your sense of reality.

Seek External Support: Talk to trusted friends, family, or professionals to validate your experiences and gain perspective.

Set Boundaries: Clearly state that manipulative behaviors are unacceptable.

Example: "I know what I experienced, and I won't discuss it further."

Rebuild Self-Confidence: Practice self-affirmation to regain trust in your abilities and judgments.

Consider Distancing: If gaslighting persists, evaluate the possibility of limiting or ending the relationship with the manipulator.

Using Knowledge of Gaslighting Ethically

Understanding gaslighting can be used to strengthen resilience against manipulations but also carries the risk of unethical application. It is crucial to use this knowledge to:

Identify Manipulators: Recognize and disarm gaslighting tactics in social or professional interactions.

Support Victims: Help those experiencing gaslighting by offering validation and guidance.

Promote Transparency: Use the knowledge to create environments where manipulation is less likely to occur.

Exercises to Recognize and Respond to Gaslighting

Reality Journal: Record events and interactions in detail to compare them with later narratives.

Confrontation Simulations: Practice responding to gaslighting tactics in a safe environment, such as with friends or in coaching sessions.

Emotional Self-Assessment: Reflect on how you feel after difficult interactions. Signs of confusion or doubt may indicate manipulation.

Ethics and Gaslighting

Using gaslighting as a deliberate tactic for unethical manipulation can cause irreparable emotional harm. It is essential to recognize ethical boundaries when applying dark psychology knowledge, protecting your integrity and the rights of others.

The Connection to Dark Psychology

Gaslighting is an advanced technique in dark psychology, demonstrating how manipulation can operate at the deepest levels of the human psyche. However, the true power of this knowledge lies in using it to disarm manipulations, protect oneself, and help others reclaim their psychological autonomy.

Understanding gaslighting is like holding a sharp knife: it can cut and destroy, or it can be used to build and protect. Mastering this technique requires not only skill but also a profound ethical responsibility.

Chapter 24
The Art of Distraction

Distraction is a subtle yet incredibly effective technique for redirecting people's attention and shaping their perception of situations. When applied strategically, it enables one to influence decisions, avoid direct confrontations, and even protect sensitive information. This chapter explores how the art of distraction can be used in personal, professional, and social contexts, detailing its psychological foundations, methods of application, and ethical boundaries for its use.

What is Distraction?

Distraction is the act of shifting attention from a primary focus to another, often less threatening or more convenient one. In terms of dark psychology, distraction is not merely a tool to avoid uncomfortable situations but a means of controlling narratives and influencing behaviors.

Why Does Distraction Work?

The effectiveness of distraction lies in how the human brain processes information:

Limited Attention Capacity

The mind can only focus on a restricted number of stimuli at a time. Redirecting attention from a specific point prevents uncomfortable issues from being deeply analyzed.

Automatic Response to New Stimuli

When something new or unexpected is presented, the brain tends to prioritize that stimulus, ignoring the previous one.

Reduction of Resistance

Distraction softens the emotional or cognitive impact of a problem, making people more susceptible to accepting solutions or changes.

Fundamental Elements of Effective Distraction

For distraction to work, it must be planned and executed precisely:

Perceived Relevance

The new focus must seem more interesting or urgent than the original.

Timing

Distraction should be introduced at the exact moment before attention fully settles on another subject.

Subtlety

Obvious distractions may be perceived as manipulations and lead to distrust.

Distraction Techniques

Below are practical techniques for effectively redirecting attention:

Introduction of a New Topic

Present a topic that immediately captures the other person's interest.

Example: During a difficult discussion, ask about a recent project or future plan relevant to the person.

Appeal to Emotions

Use an emotional stimulus to shift attention.

Example: Share a moving or funny story to break the tension in a delicate moment.

Use of Irrelevant Details

Flood the conversation with minor yet seemingly important details to shift focus.

Example: In a negotiation, emphasize logistical aspects to avoid questions about prices or deadlines.

Creation of Urgency

Introduce an issue that demands immediate attention.

Example: "We need to resolve this now before the deadline expires!"

Visual or Sensory Distraction

Present a visual or physical element that momentarily captures attention.

Example: Show graphs or images during a presentation to divert difficult questions.

Applications of Distraction in Different Contexts

The art of distraction can be strategically used in various situations:

In Negotiations

Redirect attention to secondary benefits when discussing critical points.

Example: "While we discuss the cost, don't forget about the additional benefits this package offers."

In Personal Life

Use distractions to avoid arguments or ease tensions in relationships.

Example: "Can we talk about this later? First, I want to show you something amazing I found today."

At Work

Redirect criticisms or questions to other aspects of a project.

Example: "That's valid, but I'd like to highlight the positive results we achieved this quarter."

In Social Interactions

Shift the focus of the conversation when uncomfortable topics arise.

Example: "Speaking of which, did you see the latest news about that event?"

Risks and Limitations of Distraction

While distraction is a powerful tool, it carries risks when misused:

Loss of Credibility

Distractions perceived as manipulative can damage your reputation.

Temporary Solutions

Distraction rarely resolves the underlying problem and may be seen as evasive.

Overuse

Frequent use of distractions reduces their effectiveness, as people become more alert to the technique.

Strategies to Protect Yourself from Distractions

Being able to identify and resist intentional distractions is as important as using them:

Stay Focused on the Goal

Always return to the main point of the conversation or negotiation.

Recognize Distraction Patterns

Identify when irrelevant or emotional information is being introduced to divert your attention.

Ask Direct Questions

Challenge the interlocutor to bring the focus back to the central issue.

Practical Exercises to Master Distraction

Testing Distraction Themes

In everyday conversations, introduce new topics and observe people's reactions. Adjust your approach as needed.

Redirection Simulations

Practice shifting the focus of a conversation in fictional scenarios with friends or colleagues.

Analysis of External Distractions

Study commercials, speeches, or debates to identify how distractions are used to shape perceptions.

Ethics in the Use of Distraction

As a tool of dark psychology, distraction must be used responsibly. Manipulating someone to avoid accountability or intentionally deceive is unethical. However, redirecting attention to defuse tensions or create a more favorable environment can be a positive application of this skill.

The Connection with Dark Psychology

The art of distraction is a direct application of dark psychology, exploring the limits of human attention to shape interactions and influence decisions. When used skillfully and with integrity, it enables turning challenges into opportunities and fostering more productive and harmonious interactions.

Mastering distraction means understanding that attention is a precious and limited resource. Knowing how to redirect it precisely is a skill that separates effective communicators from those who merely react to circumstances.

Chapter 25
Planting Ideas

Planting ideas in someone else's subconscious is one of the most subtle and powerful techniques of dark psychology. When done effectively, it allows you to influence thoughts, behaviors, and decisions without the target realizing they have been influenced. This chapter explores the psychological foundations of this technique, its applications, and strategies for implementing it with precision, always keeping in mind the ethical boundaries of its use.

What Does Planting Ideas Mean?

Planting an idea involves inserting a thought, belief, or suggestion into someone's subconscious indirectly, allowing them to perceive the idea as their own. This process works because the subconscious mind tends to accept repeated information or messages presented in a non-threatening way, especially when associated with emotions or familiar situations.

This technique is widely used in advertising, negotiations, leadership, and even interpersonal relationships, making it an essential element of the art of influence.

Why Does Planting Ideas Work?

Planting ideas is effective due to specific psychological factors:

The Subjective Origin Effect

When a person believes an idea is their own, they are more likely to defend it and act on it with conviction.

Subconscious Receptivity

The subconscious absorbs information more passively, especially when it is presented repeatedly or indirectly.

Emotional Association

Ideas linked to positive emotions or desirable situations are more likely to be internalized.

Reduced Resistance

By avoiding direct approaches, you reduce the likelihood of the target rejecting the idea outright.

Techniques for Planting Ideas Effectively

Planting an idea requires planning and skill. Below are practical strategies for implementing this technique:

Use Indirect Suggestions

Introduce the idea as part of a conversation or story, without making it the main focus.

Example: "I know someone who tried this approach and had great results. Maybe it could work for you too."

Tell Stories or Use Metaphors

Narratives capture attention and allow the audience to connect the suggested idea to the context.

Example: "It's like planting a seed. With patience and care, it can grow into something amazing."

Present Limited Choices

Offer options that lead to the same desired conclusion, creating the illusion of autonomy.

Example: "Would you prefer to start with a simpler plan or go straight to a comprehensive approach?"

Use Subtle Repetition

Reinforce the idea over time by introducing it in different contexts without being obvious.

Example: In various conversations, casually mention the benefits of a specific decision.

Leverage the Power of Association

Link the desired idea to something the target already values or considers positive.

Example: "This approach reminds me of your way of thinking—always innovative and strategic."

Apply Mirroring

Reflect the target's words or feelings to create a connection and increase receptiveness.

Signs That the Idea Has Been Successfully Planted

To determine if your attempt to plant an idea was successful, observe behaviors and reactions:

The target mentions the idea independently at a later time.

They show interest or curiosity about the topic without you bringing it up again.

They adopt the idea as their own, advocating for it.

Practical Applications of Idea Planting

Negotiations

Suggest solutions that indirectly benefit you, allowing the other party to perceive them as mutually advantageous.

Leadership

Inspire teams or subordinates to adopt specific strategies or goals by presenting ideas aligned with the group's values.

Interpersonal Relationships

Influence friends or family members' decisions without provoking direct resistance.

Marketing and Advertising

Position products or services as ideal solutions through stories or emotional associations.

Protecting Yourself Against Idea Planting

Just as you can use this technique, others can apply it to you. Recognizing attempts at manipulation is crucial:

Question New Ideas

Evaluate the origin of thoughts or suggestions that seem to arise spontaneously.

Identify Repetition

Notice if certain themes or messages are being introduced repeatedly in different contexts.

Seek External Perspectives

Discuss with others to gain an objective view of decisions or ideas you are considering.

Exercises to Develop the Skill of Planting Ideas

Practice Indirect Suggestions

During informal conversations, discreetly insert ideas or recommendations and observe how they are received.

Create Purposeful Stories

Develop short narratives that incorporate specific ideas or messages you want to convey.

Analyze Success Stories

Study examples of successful advertising campaigns or persuasive speeches to identify how ideas were effectively planted.

Ethical Boundaries in Idea Planting

While planting ideas is a powerful technique, using it to manipulate or deceive unethically can harm relationships and trust. Use it to:

Inspire positive changes.

Motivate people to achieve their own goals.

Resolve conflicts collaboratively.

Avoid:

Exploiting emotional vulnerabilities for personal gain.

Presenting false or misleading information.

The Connection with Dark Psychology

Planting ideas is an advanced expression of dark psychology, operating at the deepest levels of the subconscious. When used skillfully, it allows one to influence decisions almost imperceptibly, making it a powerful tool in contexts of influence and persuasion.

However, true mastery of this technique lies not only in its application but in doing so ethically, aligning your intentions with growth and mutual benefit. Planting ideas is like sowing: with patience and purpose, the fruits harvested can be transformative for both the influencer and the influenced.

Chapter 26
Creating Dependency

Creating emotional, psychological, or intellectual dependency is a sophisticated and powerful technique within dark psychology. By fostering a bond in which another person feels connected or even reliant on you for guidance, validation, or support, you can influence decisions, behaviors, and even shape their worldview. This chapter explores the foundations of this technique, strategies for applying it, and the ethical considerations that must be observed when using it.

What Is Dependency?

Dependency, in a psychological context, is a state where someone feels unable to achieve their goals or meet their needs without the help or support of another. This dependency can manifest as:

Emotional: Seeking constant validation, security, or comfort.

Psychological: Believing that decision-making or understanding the world depends on another person.

Intellectual: Relying exclusively on someone else for guidance or knowledge in a specific area.

While creating dependency can be a powerful tool of influence, it must be used responsibly, as unethical manipulation can cause lasting harm.

Why Creating Dependency Works

Dependency arises from fundamental human needs such as connection, security, and guidance. Reasons for its effectiveness include:

The Search for Support
People naturally seek reliable sources of help in moments of uncertainty or vulnerability.

Positive Reinforcement
By consistently offering support, you become a trusted presence, strengthening the bond.

Fear of Loss
When someone becomes emotionally or psychologically dependent, the fear of losing that connection increases their susceptibility to influence.

Familiarity and Repetition
The more frequently someone seeks your support, the deeper the cycle of dependency becomes.Techniques for Effectively Creating Dependency
Creating dependency requires a careful balance between providing genuine support and establishing a bond of influence. Here are practical strategies:

Be a Reliable Source of Support
Be available in times of need, demonstrating empathy and understanding.
Example: "Whenever you need someone to listen, you can count on me."

Offer Unique Solutions
Position yourself as someone with the answers or skills the other person needs.
Example: "I know a method that can solve exactly that problem."

Create Interaction Routines
Encourage regular interactions, establishing a pattern of contact that reinforces the connection.
Example: "Let's meet every week to discuss how you're progressing."

Reinforce the Value of the Connection
Praise and value the relationship, making the other person see the bond as indispensable.

Example: "Our partnership has been so positive; it's amazing what we've achieved together."

Provide Consistent Validation

Affirm the other person's feelings or decisions to strengthen their trust in you.

Example: "You made the right decision. That was very wise of you."

Show Yourself as Indispensable in Crucial Moments

Support the person during challenging situations, creating an association between you and overcoming difficulties.

Example: "I'm here to help you solve this, just like we always do together."

Signs Dependency Has Been Established

Certain behaviors can indicate that dependency is in place:

The person consults you before making important decisions.

They consistently seek your validation or approval.

They exhibit discomfort or anxiety when you are unavailable.

They frequently refer to you as an essential figure in their life.

Applications of Dependency in Different Contexts

Personal Relationships

Creating emotional dependency can strengthen bonds, but it must be balanced to avoid power imbalances.

Professional Environments

Positioning yourself as an indispensable source of knowledge or support can increase your influence at work.

Marketing and Sales

Brands often create emotional dependency by linking products to values or emotional needs.

Example: Products that promote slogans like "You deserve the best" or "Your life simplified."

Leadership

Effective leaders often create intellectual dependency, being seen as reliable guides in times of uncertainty.

Risks and Limits of Creating Dependency

Although effective, creating dependency carries risks if not used responsibly:

Unbalanced Relationships

A bond based solely on dependency can lead to resentment or a loss of autonomy.

Emotional Burnout

Being a constant source of support can be emotionally draining.

Unethical Manipulation

Exploiting dependency for personal gain can cause psychological harm to others.

Strategies to Avoid Becoming Dependent

It is equally important to protect yourself from being placed in a state of dependency:

Cultivate Autonomy

Seek information and make decisions based on your own judgment, consulting other sources.

Recognize Patterns of Control

Identify if someone is intentionally creating dependency to limit your independence.

Strengthen Your Skills

Invest in personal development to reduce the need for external support.

Exercises to Practice Creating Dependency

Interaction Diary

Record how you provide support and observe if people begin to seek you out regularly.

Support Simulations

Practice being a source of validation or guidance in hypothetical scenarios with friends or colleagues.

Study Role Models

Analyze leaders or influential figures to understand how they create emotional or intellectual dependency in their followers.

Ethics in Creating Dependency

Creating dependency should be done with ethical intent, fostering mutual growth rather than exploitation. Use this technique to:

Support people in difficult times.

Help others develop skills or confidence in themselves.

Build meaningful and mutually beneficial connections.

Avoid:

Using dependency to unfairly control or manipulate.

Encouraging long-term dependency instead of promoting autonomy.

The Connection to Dark Psychology

Creating dependency is a classic example of dark psychology, demonstrating how emotional and psychological needs can be used to influence behavior. When applied effectively, this technique can build strong relationships and increase your influence, but it should always be used with care and responsibility.

Mastering this skill is not just about gaining power but also about creating bonds based on trust, respect, and genuine support. Dependency, when balanced, can be transformative for both the influencer and the influenced.

Chapter 27
Recognizing Manipulators

The ability to recognize manipulators is essential for maintaining your psychological and emotional autonomy. In a world where social interactions often involve attempts at influence, being able to identify manipulative tactics protects you from exploitation and strengthens your resilience. This chapter explores the characteristic traits of manipulators, their most common techniques, and strategies to shield yourself from their influence.

Who Are Manipulators?

Manipulators are individuals who use psychological or emotional tactics to control or influence others, often to achieve personal gains. They can be found in any sphere of life—at work, in personal relationships, or even in larger social settings.

Although not all manipulators act with malicious intent, their actions can cause emotional and psychological harm, especially when exercised persistently and unethically.

Common Traits of Manipulators

Manipulators tend to exhibit certain traits that make them easily recognizable:

Communication Skills

They are articulate and use language to confuse, persuade, or divert attention.

Instrumental Empathy

They show empathy only to identify vulnerabilities and exploit them.

Focus on Personal Gains

Manipulators often prioritize their own interests over others, even if it involves deceit or exploitation.

Behavioral Shifts

They adapt their attitudes or strategies depending on whom they are trying to influence.

Avoidance of Responsibility

They evade accountability, often blaming others for problems.

Common Manipulation Tactics

To recognize manipulators, it's crucial to understand the tactics they frequently employ:

Guilt and Emotional Blackmail

They make the victim feel guilty to get what they want.

Example: "After everything I've done for you, this is how you treat me?"

Gaslighting

They distance the victim from their own perception of reality, causing self-doubt.

Criticism Disguised as Advice

They use supposedly constructive comments to undermine the victim's confidence.

Example: "I'm only saying this because I care, but you really need to improve in this area."

Silent Treatment or Withdrawal

Manipulators may withdraw emotionally or physically to pressure the victim into compliance.

Example: Ignoring messages or avoiding important conversations as a form of control.

Empty Promises

They make promises they rarely fulfill to keep the other person waiting or hopeful.

Confusion Tactics

They introduce contradictory information or change positions to disorient the victim.

How to Recognize a Manipulator in Action

To identify manipulators in your life, watch for the following signs:

You often feel guilt or confusion after interacting with them.

There's a pattern of emotional or mental manipulation in your interactions.

The person frequently changes their stance or avoids directly answering your questions.

Your decisions are influenced by their needs or desires, even against your will.

Impacts of Manipulators on Victims

Manipulation can cause a range of negative effects, such as:

Loss of Self-Confidence

The victim may start doubting their own judgment.

Social Isolation

Manipulators often distance the victim from their support networks.

Stress and Anxiety

The constant pressure to please or comply can lead to emotional exhaustion.

Psychological Dependence

The victim may become reliant on the manipulator for guidance or validation.

Strategies for Dealing with Manipulators

Recognizing manipulators is only the first step; knowing how to deal with them is crucial for protecting your autonomy.

Set Clear Boundaries

Be firm about what you will and will not accept in interactions.

Example: "I'm not comfortable with that kind of comment. Please don't do it again."

Question Motivations

Ask yourself what the manipulator might gain from certain actions or behaviors.

Avoid Emotional Reactions
Manipulators often feed on emotional responses. Respond calmly and objectively.

Seek External Validation
Consult trusted friends or advisors to confirm if your perceptions are accurate.

Be Direct
Confront the manipulator with clear evidence of their behavior.

Example: "I've noticed you've changed your mind on this several times. Could you clarify your position?"

Consider Distancing Yourself
In cases where manipulation is persistent and harmful, limiting or ending contact may be necessary.

Exercises to Practice Identifying Manipulators

Case Studies
Analyze characters from movies or books known for being manipulative and identify the tactics they use.

Self-Reflection
Review past interactions where you felt uncomfortable or pressured, looking for signs of manipulation.

Confrontation Simulations
Practice responding to manipulative situations with a friend or coach to improve your assertiveness.

Protecting Yourself Long-Term
Beyond handling specific situations, adopt practices to strengthen your resilience:

Build Self-Esteem
The more confident you are in your abilities and decisions, the less susceptible you'll be to manipulation.

Develop Critical Thinking
Analyze information and situations before reacting impulsively.

Create a Support Network
Surround yourself with trusted people who can validate your perceptions and offer emotional support.

Ethics in Identifying Manipulators

While recognizing manipulators is important, do not use these skills to unfairly or unethically manipulate others. The goal should be to protect your integrity and, when possible, help others develop healthier, more transparent relationships.

The Connection to Dark Psychology

Recognizing manipulators is an essential component of dark psychology, as it empowers you to identify external influences and preserve your autonomy. This skill not only protects you from harm but also enhances your ability to navigate complex social and professional interactions with confidence.

Mastering this skill means understanding that the power over your mind is yours, and recognizing manipulators is the first step to keeping it.

Chapter 28
The Role of Reverse Psychology

Reverse psychology is a technique that leverages people's natural resistance to influence their decisions or actions. Instead of persuading them directly, it involves suggesting the opposite of what is desired, relying on their reaction to the initial suggestion to adopt the preferred position or action. This chapter explores the fundamentals of reverse psychology, its psychological basis, ways to apply it, and the ethical considerations necessary to use it responsibly and effectively.

What is Reverse Psychology?

Reverse psychology is a form of influence based on the principle of psychological reactance. This concept suggests that people have an innate aversion to feeling their freedom of choice is being restricted, prompting them to resist direct commands or suggestions, often opting to do the exact opposite.

Why Does Reverse Psychology Work?

The effectiveness of this technique is grounded in three main factors:

Psychological Reactance

When a direct suggestion or command is perceived as a threat to autonomy, people tend to act against it to reaffirm their independence.

Desire for Control

Individuals enjoy feeling in control of their decisions. Reverse psychology capitalizes on this desire, creating the impression that the final decision was made autonomously.

Curiosity and Contradiction

Suggesting the opposite stimulates curiosity about what would happen if the suggestion were challenged, encouraging exploration of that possibility.

When to Use Reverse Psychology

While powerful, reverse psychology is most effective in specific contexts:

Rebellious or Stubborn Individuals

People who resist direct orders or have a strong desire for independence are more susceptible to this technique.

Children or Adolescents

Young people often challenge authority figures to assert their autonomy, making reverse psychology useful in educational or parental contexts.

Low-Risk Decisions

In situations where the outcome is not critical, reverse psychology can direct behavior with minimal resistance.

Techniques for Applying Reverse Psychology

Reverse psychology should be applied subtly to avoid making the target aware they are being manipulated. Here are some effective strategies:

Contradictory Suggestion

State the opposite of what you truly desire, casually and non-imposingly.

Example: "I don't think you'd enjoy this movie; it's a bit different from your style."

Apparent Limitation

Highlight restrictions or obstacles to make the desired option more appealing.

Example: "You probably wouldn't want to sign up for this course now; it requires a lot of commitment."

Choice Redirection

Offer options where the one you prefer seems initially less desirable.

Example: "Choose whatever you want for dinner, but I imagine you'd prefer something simpler today."

Negative Framing

Present the desired behavior as unlikely or difficult, encouraging the person to prove you wrong.

Example: "I doubt you can finish this task as quickly as you think."

Reinforcement of Choice Freedom

Emphasize that the final decision is up to the person, strengthening their sense of control.

Example: "Of course, it's your choice. But I don't think this is the best option for you right now."

Practical Examples of Reverse Psychology

Child Education

To encourage a child to eat vegetables: "I'm not sure if you're ready to try these broccoli; they're for kids who like more grown-up food."

Marketing

Stores use phrases like "Exclusive offer for a limited time!" to create urgency and attract customers.

Interpersonal Relationships

In discussions, disarm resistance by saying: "I understand why you wouldn't want to do this right now."

Cautions and Limits of Reverse Psychology

While effective, the use of reverse psychology comes with risks and limitations:

Excessive Use

Overusing it can lead to distrust as people begin to notice the pattern.

Opposite Outcomes

In some situations, especially with highly analytical individuals, the technique can fail or produce undesired results.

Relational Impact

Constant manipulation through reverse psychology can harm relationships, fostering an atmosphere of distrust.

Strategies to Protect Against Reverse Psychology

Just as it's important to know how to apply it, it's crucial to safeguard yourself from its misuse:

Recognize the Context

Be aware of contradictory suggestions or apparent limitations that may be attempts to influence your decisions.

Analyze Your Motivations

Ask yourself why you're reacting a certain way to a suggestion or restriction.

Stay Focused on Your Goals

Make decisions based on your interests and objectives rather than responding to provocations or challenges.

Exercises to Practice Reverse Psychology

Test in Everyday Conversations

Insert contradictory suggestions in casual dialogues and observe reactions.

Create Hypothetical Scenarios

Plan reverse psychology strategies for specific situations and practice their application in simulations.

Study Real-Life Examples

Analyze marketing campaigns, interactions in movies, or political speeches to identify the use of reverse psychology.

Ethics in the Application of Reverse Psychology

Reverse psychology is a powerful technique but should be used with care to avoid violating ethical principles. Use it to:

Promote positive decisions or behaviors.

Reduce conflicts or defuse tense situations.

Encourage personal or professional growth.

Avoid:

Manipulating for personal gain at others' expense.

Applying it to critical decisions or situations that may cause emotional or material harm.

Connection to Dark Psychology

Reverse psychology exemplifies how the human mind can be subtly influenced by leveraging natural resistance and the desire for autonomy. When used responsibly, it allows for effective influence without resorting to direct confrontation, making it a valuable tool in social and professional interactions.

Mastering reverse psychology is more than a persuasion skill—it is the art of understanding and working with human reactions, creating opportunities for connection and understanding in challenging situations.

Chapter 29
Dealing with Resistance

Resistance is a natural reaction when people feel their ideas, beliefs, or freedom are being challenged. Knowing how to manage this resistance is crucial to maintaining control in interactions, fostering cooperation, and achieving goals without unnecessary confrontations. This chapter explores the reasons behind resistance, how to identify it, and the most effective psychological techniques to overcome it.

What is Resistance?

Resistance is the opposition or reluctance to accept or follow an idea, proposal, or change. It can be passive, such as refusing to cooperate, or active, like direct confrontation.

Resistance mainly stems from three sources:

Fear of Loss

Resistance arises when a person believes that accepting something will result in the loss of control, security, or personal advantages.

Distrust

When there is no trust in the messenger or message, people tend to reject proposals or ideas, even if they are beneficial.

Deep-Rooted Convictions

Strongly held beliefs and values generate resistance to ideas that challenge or contradict them.

How to Identify Resistance

Recognizing signs of resistance is the first step in addressing it. These signs may include:

Non-Verbal Responses
Folding arms, avoiding eye contact, or adopting a defensive posture.

Repetitive Argumentation
Repeating the same arguments, even after they have been addressed.

Topic Changes
Shifting the subject or avoiding the main discussion.

Prolonged Silence
Choosing silence over direct responses as a way to avoid confrontation.

Psychological Strategies to Overcome Resistance
Overcoming resistance isn't about force but about understanding and persuasion. Below are effective techniques to manage this barrier:

Build Rapport Before Moving Forward
Establish a genuine connection before presenting ideas. When people feel understood and respected, they are more receptive.

Example: "I understand where you're coming from and appreciate your perspective."

Validate Emotions and Beliefs
Acknowledge the other person's feelings or concerns without invalidating them.

Example: "It's natural to feel hesitant about something new. It shows you're thinking carefully."

Use the Power of Questions
Instead of arguing directly, ask questions that encourage the person to reconsider their position.

Example: "What do you think would happen if we tried this approach for a short period?"

Offer Small Concessions
Start with minor requests or changes that don't feel threatening, gradually building acceptance.

Example: "How about we try this idea in a limited scenario to see how it works?"

Reframe the Problem

Reformulate the situation to emphasize the benefits or reduce negative perceptions.

Example: Instead of "We're changing your routine," say, "We're adjusting your routine to make it more efficient."

Introduce Alternatives

Provide options to give the person a sense of control, even if all choices align with your goal.

Example: "Would you prefer starting with this approach or exploring another idea first?"

Overcoming Emotional Resistance

When resistance is rooted in strong emotions like fear or frustration, specific techniques can help:

Active Empathy

Show understanding by echoing the person's concerns and demonstrating recognition.

Example: "It seems like you're worried about how this will affect your time. Is that right?"

Calm Responses

Maintain a calm and confident tone to diffuse negative emotions and create a more receptive environment.

Focus on Positive Outcomes

Highlight the emotional or practical benefits of acceptance.

Example: "This might feel challenging now, but imagine how relieved you'll feel once we resolve this issue."

Managing Intellectual Resistance

Intellectual resistance arises when someone disagrees with an idea or proposal based on logic or facts. To address this:

Present Relevant Data

Use clear information and evidence to support your position.

Acknowledge Strengths in the Opposing Argument

Admitting merit in the other person's view shows respect and makes them more open to listening.

Example: "You're right about the challenges involved. That's why I believe this approach might work better."

Draw Comparisons

Objectively compare your proposal with alternatives to demonstrate its advantages.

Applications of Dark Psychology in Managing Resistance

Dark psychology provides valuable insights into overcoming resistance:

Reading Body Language

Identify non-verbal cues of resistance to adjust your approach in real time.

Idea Planting

Introduce your proposal indirectly to minimize initial barriers.

Exploiting Confirmation Bias

Leverage the person's existing beliefs to reinforce the merits of your idea.

Example: "You mentioned valuing efficiency. This solution is exactly about that."

Common Mistakes in Dealing with Resistance

Avoiding mistakes is as important as applying the right strategies. Here are behaviors that can exacerbate resistance:

Being Confrontational or Authoritarian

Forcing someone to accept your position increases resistance rather than reducing it.

Ignoring Emotions

Failing to acknowledge emotional concerns makes the person feel undervalued.

Reacting Impatiently

Rushing acceptance can breed distrust and rejection.

Exercises to Practice Resistance Management

Conflict Simulations

Practice managing resistance in simulated scenarios, adjusting your approach based on responses.

Analyze Past Conversations

Review previous interactions where resistance occurred and identify how you could have responded more effectively.

Roleplay with Friends

Train to address common objections by focusing on validating feelings and redirecting the conversation.

Ethics in Resistance Management

When overcoming resistance, it's essential to respect the other person's autonomy. Use these techniques to:

Build consensus that benefits both parties.

Promote growth and learning.

Resolve conflicts constructively.

Avoid:

Manipulating for personal gain at others' expense.

Ignoring the other person's boundaries or values.

Connection to Dark Psychology

Dealing with resistance exemplifies how dark psychology can be used to dismantle barriers and foster cooperation. This skill not only enhances your effectiveness in social and professional interactions but also promotes healthier and more productive connections.

Mastering resistance management is more than overcoming objections—it's about building bridges, creating understanding, and transforming challenges into opportunities for growth and collaboration.

Chapter 30
The Power of Silence

Silence, often underestimated, is one of the most powerful tools in dark psychology. When used strategically, it can defuse conflicts, create tension, manipulate social dynamics, and even induce desired behaviors without the need for words. This chapter explores how silence can be used to influence people, control situations, and strengthen your presence in personal and professional interactions.

The Meaning of Silence in Psychology

Silence goes beyond the absence of sound; it communicates intentions, creates spaces for reflection, and amplifies the perception of power and control. In contexts of influence, silence is an active tool that allows you to shape the environment and direct interactions.

Why Is Silence So Effective?

Silence works because it challenges human expectations in social interactions. Most people feel uncomfortable with prolonged silence, leading them to fill the space with words or actions that reveal thoughts, intentions, or weaknesses.

Creates Tension

Silence can heighten pressure in negotiation or conflict situations, forcing the other party to act.

Demonstrates Control

Those who master silence exude calm, confidence, and authority.

Amplifies Meaning

Silent pauses emphasize what was said before or create anticipation for what will be said next.

Induces Reflection

Silence encourages the interlocutor to think deeply about what was discussed, allowing ideas to take root in their mind.

Techniques for Using Silence as an Influence Tool

Silence can be applied in various ways to manipulate social dynamics and achieve desired outcomes.

Strategic Silence in Negotiations

After presenting a proposal or objection, remain silent and let the other party fill the void. This often leads to unexpected concessions or clarifications.

Example: "Our offer is 20%. [Prolonged silence]"

Dramatic Pause

Use silence immediately after a striking statement to let it resonate and gain weight.

Example: "This is the opportunity you've been waiting for... [silence]"

Reflective Silence

During a discussion or conflict, use silence to demonstrate that you are carefully considering your response. This conveys maturity and credibility.

Silence as Disarmament

When faced with criticism or verbal attacks, silence can disarm the aggressor, leaving them uncertain about their position.

Example: Allow the other person to finish speaking without interruption and respond with a thoughtful pause.

Silence to Establish Authority

In meetings or presentations, use silence before you begin speaking to capture attention and establish presence.

Silence as Isolation

Emotionally or physically withdraw from an interaction to highlight its significance or force the other person to reflect.

Example: Abruptly end a conversation with a silent gesture and leave the room.

Applications of Silence in Different Contexts

Negotiations
Silence can create pressure or convey confidence, compelling the other party to reconsider their stance.

Conflicts
In tense situations, silence helps avoid impulsive reactions, allowing you to regain emotional and strategic control.

Personal Relationships
Silent pauses during discussions can reduce emotional escalation and create space for mutual understanding.

Leadership and Management
Leaders who use silence wisely project authority and encourage deeper reflection within their teams.

Risks and Limits of Using Silence
Although silence is a powerful tool, it must be used carefully to avoid unwanted side effects:

Perception of Coldness or Disinterest
Excessive silence can be interpreted as a lack of empathy or engagement.

Loss of Connection
In emotional contexts, silence can create barriers rather than promote understanding.

Reverse Effects with Dominant Individuals
With highly assertive people, silence may be perceived as weakness or tacit agreement.

Strategies to Resist Silence Used Against You
Just as you can use it, others may employ silence as an influence tool. To protect yourself:

Recognize the Psychological Game
Be aware that silence may be intentional and maintain confidence in your position.

Fill the Silence with Questions
Strengthen your position by steering the conversation with questions that require answers.

Example: "Do you have any specific concerns about this?"

Use Silence as a Countermeasure

When confronted with silence, respond calmly with calculated pauses to balance the dynamic.

Exercises to Master the Use of Silence

Practice Pauses

In everyday conversations, introduce strategic pauses after important statements and observe reactions.

Negotiation Simulations

Train using silence in simulated negotiations, allowing the other party to respond first.

Reaction Control

In discussions or criticisms, practice responding with silence before articulating a thoughtful reply.

Ethics in Using Silence

Like all dark psychology techniques, silence should be used ethically. Use it to:

Promote clarity and reflection in discussions.

Create space for collaborative solutions.

Avoid unnecessary confrontations or emotional escalation.

Avoid:

Using silence to emotionally manipulate or deliberately cause distress.

Withdrawing from important situations without resolving key issues.

The Connection with Dark Psychology

Silence exemplifies the power of restraint and strategy in human interactions. It is not merely the absence of words but a tool that can shape perceptions, influence decisions, and create balance in complex situations.

Mastering the use of silence means understanding that, in many interactions, less can be more. When used wisely, silence becomes a powerful ally, allowing you to control the narrative without saying a single word.

Chapter 31
Subtle Intimidation

Subtle intimidation is a refined influence technique that does not rely on explicit fear but uses gestures, behaviors, and implicit messages to establish control and authority in interactions. When applied correctly, it can create an environment of respect, guide behaviors, and deter opposition—all without appearing as a direct threat. This chapter explores the psychological foundations of subtle intimidation, its applications, and the ethical considerations required to use it responsibly.

What Is Subtle Intimidation?

Subtle intimidation involves the deliberate use of behaviors and nonverbal cues to communicate strength, power, or dominance indirectly. Rather than inciting direct fear, it fosters a perception of control or authority, encouraging others to cooperate or yield.

Unlike aggressive intimidation, which may provoke resistance or hostility, subtle intimidation aims to secure compliance without harming relationships or creating unnecessary tension.

Why Does Subtle Intimidation Work?

Its effectiveness is rooted in social psychology and nonverbal communication. People often respond more to the subtext of an interaction than to spoken words, being influenced by:

Presence and Behavior

A confident posture and controlled gestures convey authority without words.

Controlled Ambiguity

Implicit or indirect messages create just enough uncertainty to discourage challenges or resistance.

Social and Hierarchical Pressure

The perception that someone holds power or control prompts others to adjust their behavior to avoid conflict.

The Impact of Nonverbal Communication

Studies show that nonverbal communication can be more impactful than words, especially in contexts involving power dynamics.

Techniques of Subtle Intimidation

Applying subtle intimidation requires a balance between assertiveness and emotional control. Below are effective techniques to employ it:

Authoritative Posture

Adopt an upright posture with relaxed shoulders and feet firmly planted. This conveys stability and strength.

Firm Eye Contact

Maintain steady eye contact without looking away to exude confidence and presence.

Example: During a challenging conversation, look directly into the other person's eyes while they speak.

Strategic Silence

Use intentional pauses to create tension and emphasize your position.

Example: Pause before responding to an objection, creating anticipation.

Controlled Tone of Voice

A calm and firm tone is more intimidating than shouting or aggressive speech.

Calculated Gestures

Slow and deliberate movements signal self-control and confidence. Avoid excessive or nervous gestures.

Choice of Words

Use assertive language, avoiding words that sound hesitant or uncertain.

Example: Replace "I think we could try this" with "We will adopt this approach."

Controlled Proximity

In appropriate situations, slightly reduce the physical distance to reinforce your presence without invading personal space.

Practical Examples of Subtle Intimidation

In the Workplace

During a meeting, maintain a firm posture and use pauses before speaking to establish your position as a leader without direct imposition.

In Negotiations

Allow silence to dominate after presenting an offer, creating enough discomfort for the other party to reconsider.

In Social Interactions

A controlled smile and direct gaze during a challenging conversation can convey confidence and disarm the other person.

Advantages of Subtle Intimidation

Preserves Relationships: By avoiding direct confrontations, it maintains an environment of mutual respect.

Reduces Resistance: The lack of explicit threat minimizes the likelihood of defensive reactions.

Projects Natural Authority: Strengthens your presence without resorting to aggressive or excessive behaviors.

Risks and Limitations of Subtle Intimidation

Overuse: Frequent application may be perceived as manipulative or cold, damaging relationships.

Misinterpretation: Nonverbal cues can be misunderstood, leading to unexpected reactions.

Impact on Sensitive Individuals: Those who are more sensitive may feel uncomfortable or alienated, even if the technique is well-intentioned.

Strategies to Resist Subtle Intimidation

If you find yourself targeted by subtle intimidation, there are strategies to balance the dynamic:

Recognize the Intent
Identify the behaviors as attempts at influence and stay focused on the facts.

Project Confidence
Respond with equally assertive behaviors, such as maintaining eye contact and a firm posture.

Break the Rhythm
Use humor or change the subject to defuse tension and reset the interaction's dynamic.

Ask Direct Questions
Forcing the other person to articulate their intentions can dissolve the aura of control.
Example: "Can you clarify what you meant by that?"

Exercises to Develop Subtle Intimidation
Practice Authoritative Postures
Rehearse postures and expressions in front of a mirror to convey confidence.

Control Silence
Introduce strategic pauses in casual conversations and observe reactions.

Simulate Challenging Situations
Practice complex interactions with friends or colleagues to refine your ability to project subtle authority.

Ethics in Subtle Intimidation
Like all tools of dark psychology, subtle intimidation must be used responsibly. Use it to:

Strengthen your position in professional or social situations.

Protect yourself against manipulation or disrespect.

Promote conflict resolution without open confrontations.

Avoid:

Using it to exploit or intimidate vulnerable individuals.

Relying on it as a means of absolute control or oppression.

The Connection with Dark Psychology
Subtle intimidation is a sophisticated example of dark psychology, showcasing how small adjustments in posture,

language, and behavior can create significant impacts in social and professional interactions.

Mastering this technique goes beyond learning to exert influence—it's about balancing power, respect, and empathy to build authentic and productive connections.

Chapter 32
The Psychology of Reciprocity

Reciprocity is a powerful principle of psychology that governs human interactions and shapes behaviors. It is based on people's natural tendency to return favors, gestures, or concessions, creating a sense of social obligation. When applied strategically, the principle of reciprocity can influence decisions, build relationships, and shape power dynamics. This chapter explores the fundamentals of the psychology of reciprocity, ways to use it, and the ethical implications of its application.

What Is the Principle of Reciprocity?

Reciprocity is the foundation of many social and cultural systems, widely recognized as a cornerstone of human interactions. The principle is simple: when someone does something for you, there is an implicit pressure to return the gesture.

This phenomenon is so universal that it transcends cultures, being found in both modern and traditional societies. Reciprocity not only strengthens social connections but can also be used to subtly influence behaviors.

Why Does Reciprocity Work?

The effectiveness of reciprocity is rooted in social norms and psychological mechanisms:

Social Pressure

People dislike being seen as ungrateful, which motivates them to return favors.

Desire for Balance

Reciprocity creates a sense of justice in interactions, balancing the act of giving and receiving.

Obligation Bias

Receiving something generates a feeling of obligation, often unconscious, to return the favor, even if the initial gesture was small.

Connection Building

Reciprocity strengthens social bonds, creating a positive cycle of cooperation.

Techniques for Using the Principle of Reciprocity

Offer Value First

Begin the interaction by offering something genuine, such as help, a gift, or valuable information.

Example: In negotiations, present an initial concession to stimulate reciprocity.

Create Small Gestures of Generosity

Small, unexpected favors can have a significant psychological impact.

Example: Sending a personalized thank-you note after a meeting.

Use Strategic Concessions

Make an initial concession to create a sense of obligation in the other party.

Example: Offering an additional discount to encourage a quick purchase decision.

Reinforce Gratitude

After receiving something, acknowledge the gesture to increase the likelihood of reciprocation.

Example: "Thank you so much for your help. It made all the difference for me."

Create Memorable Experiences

Offer something meaningful or personalized that will be remembered and reinforce the obligation to reciprocate.

Example: Providing an exclusive gift at a corporate event.

Practical Applications of Reciprocity

Negotiations

Initial concessions can prompt the other party to make similar concessions, facilitating favorable agreements.

Marketing and Sales

Free samples, gifts, or valuable content create a sense of obligation that increases the chances of conversion.

Example: Offering a free trial of software to encourage later purchase.

Personal Relationships

Small acts of kindness or support strengthen relationships and encourage emotional reciprocity.

Leadership

Leaders who proactively help their teams often receive greater commitment and loyalty in return.

Risks and Limitations of Using Reciprocity

Perceived Manipulation

Gestures may be interpreted as manipulative if they seem overly calculated.

Resistance to Obligation

Some people may reject reciprocity if they feel pressured or exploited.

Context Dependence

Reciprocity is less effective in situations where social norms are weak or absent.

Recognizing Reciprocity Used Against You

Just as you can use this principle, it's important to identify when it is being applied to influence you:

Unexpected Favors: Consider whether a received favor comes with an implicit expectation of return.

Intentional Concessions: Reflect on whether offered concessions are meant to induce a response.

Excessive Generosity: Be wary of gestures that appear overly altruistic or disproportionate.

Strategies to Resist Manipulative Reciprocity

Recognize the Context: Assess the intention behind the gesture and question whether it is genuine or strategic.

Set Boundaries: Accept gestures or favors only when you are comfortable not reciprocating immediately.

Express Gratitude Without Commitment: Show appreciation without creating an obligation to return.

Example: "Thank you so much, but I can't guarantee I'll be able to return the favor at the same level right now."

Exercises to Master the Use of Reciprocity

Offer Simple Favors: Practice small acts of generosity and observe how people respond.

Create Concessions in Simulations: In fictitious scenarios, try making initial concessions and analyze how they influence others' behavior.

Study Examples: Examine marketing campaigns or famous negotiations that utilized reciprocity as a tool.

Ethics in the Application of Reciprocity

Reciprocity is a powerful technique, but it must be used ethically to avoid exploitation or manipulation. Use it to:

Build authentic relationships.

Promote mutually beneficial solutions.

Establish connections based on trust and cooperation.

Avoid:

Demanding disproportionate returns.

Using the principle to exploit emotional or financial vulnerabilities.

The Connection to Dark Psychology

The psychology of reciprocity is a subtle yet effective tool, demonstrating how small actions can trigger significant responses. When used ethically, it fosters deeper relationships and influences behaviors without causing resistance or discomfort.

Mastering the principle of reciprocity means understanding that giving and receiving are not isolated acts but part of a social cycle that, when applied correctly, transforms interactions into opportunities for connection and mutual growth.

Chapter 33
Recognizing Falsehoods

The ability to recognize falsehoods is one of the most valuable skills in the arsenal of dark psychology. Identifying lies, omissions, and inconsistencies in people's words and behaviors allows you to make informed decisions, avoid manipulation, and maintain an advantage in social and professional interactions. This chapter explores techniques, signs, and strategies for detecting falsehoods effectively and ethically.

What Is Falsehood?

Falsehood is any form of intentional communication that distorts or omits the truth. It can take different forms:

Direct Lies

Statements that intentionally contradict facts.

Example: "I didn't go to the event yesterday" when the person was clearly present.

Omissions

Failing to mention relevant information to lead to a false conclusion.

Example: Not disclosing a significant flaw in a report.

Inconsistencies

Contradictions in stories or explanations that suggest an attempt to cover the truth.

Deceptive Behaviors

Body language, tone of voice, or expressions that do not align with spoken words.

Why Do People Lie?

Lying is common behavior and occurs for various reasons, including:

Avoiding Consequences: To escape punishment or criticism.

Protecting Image: To preserve reputation or appear more competent.

Manipulating Situations: To gain an advantage or deceive others.

Facilitating Social Interactions: Social lies, such as false compliments, aim to avoid conflict or embarrassment.

Common Signs of Falsehood

Although detecting lies with absolute precision is difficult, certain signs may indicate deceit:

Changes in Behavior

The person may become restless, avoid eye contact, or exaggerate facial expressions to appear sincere. Inconsistencies in the Story

Details that change over time or contradictory responses indicate the truth might be distorted.

Pauses and Hesitations

Lies often require more time to construct, resulting in pauses before responding.

Contradictory Body Language

Gestures that do not align with spoken words, such as denying something while nodding affirmatively.

Excessive or Sparse Details

Some people include irrelevant details to make lies convincing, while others provide vague responses to avoid contradictions.

Techniques for Recognizing Falsehoods

Observe Microexpressions

Quick, involuntary facial expressions can reveal true emotions that contradict spoken words.

Example: A fake smile can be identified by the lack of muscle contraction around the eyes.

Analyze Tone of Voice

Changes in tone or speech rhythm may indicate nervousness or discomfort associated with lying.

Ask Direct and Repeated Questions

Inquire about the same details at different times to uncover inconsistencies.

Example: "Can you explain again what happened before the meeting?"

Watch for Evasive Responses

Liars often avoid direct answers by changing the subject or providing generic replies.

Establish a Behavioral Baseline

Observe how the person behaves in normal situations to identify changes during suspicious interactions.

Use Strategic Silence

After asking a direct question, remain silent. This can pressure the person to reveal more than intended.

Applications of Recognizing Falsehoods

Negotiations

Identifying when the other party is exaggerating or lying about their position can give you a significant advantage.

Personal Relationships

Knowing when someone is hiding something important helps maintain trust-based relationships.

Workplace

Detecting falsehoods in reports or communications prevents poor decisions and protects against manipulation.

Risks of Detecting Falsehoods

While recognizing falsehoods is valuable, it can present risks:

False Positives: Misinterpreting signals as lies can harm relationships.

Negative Reactions: Accusing someone of lying may provoke defensiveness or conflict.

Excessive Skepticism: Becoming overly distrustful can erode your ability to build genuine connections.

How to Protect Yourself from Falsehoods

Beyond identifying lies, it is essential to take steps to protect yourself from them:

Validate Information: Always seek evidence or corroboration to verify the truth of statements.

Use Contracts or Documentation: In professional contexts, formalize agreements to avoid misunderstandings or intentional deception.

Develop Emotional Awareness: Train yourself to recognize how lies affect you emotionally, helping maintain clarity during interactions.

Set Boundaries: Confront dishonest behaviors assertively to discourage future falsehoods.

Exercises to Practice Detecting Falsehoods

Watch Interviews: Analyze public interviews or debates, observing inconsistencies or nonverbal signals.

Simulations with Friends: Practice detecting lies in "truth or lie" games with friends.

Study Real-Life Cases: Analyze famous events where lies were uncovered to understand patterns of behavior.

Ethics in Recognizing Falsehoods

Using this skill ethically is essential. While identifying lies protects you from manipulation, it should not be used to exploit or humiliate others.

Use this skill to:

Protect yourself from deception or abuse.

Build trust in interactions based on truth.

Resolve conflicts constructively by bringing the truth to light.

Avoid:

Publicly exposing falsehoods unnecessarily to embarrass someone.

Using knowledge of lies for blackmail or manipulation.

The Connection to Dark Psychology

Recognizing falsehoods is a core skill in dark psychology, enabling you to navigate social and professional interactions with clarity and precision. This ability not only strengthens your resilience against manipulation but also enhances your influence by establishing yourself as trustworthy and perceptive.

Mastering this skill is like sharpening a blade: it must be used with care and purpose, protecting yourself and those around you from harmful deception and lies.

Chapter 34
The Importance of Timing

Timing is the art of acting at the right moment, leveraging ideal conditions to maximize impact and effectiveness. In dark psychology, timing plays a crucial role in applying techniques of influence, manipulation, and persuasion. Knowing when to speak, act, or even wait can mean the difference between success and failure in social interactions, negotiations, and other contexts. This chapter explores how to identify the right moment, why it is essential, and how to use it strategically to achieve your goals.

What is Timing?

Timing refers to the ability to synchronize actions or words with the most opportune moment to achieve the desired effect. It is intrinsically linked to the perception of the environment, the emotional state of the people involved, and the natural flow of events.

In dark psychology, timing is used to:

Increase Receptiveness

Choosing the right moment to present an idea or suggestion increases the chances of it being accepted.

Minimize Resistance

Acting when the other party's defenses are down reduces the likelihood of objections.

Maximize Impact

Messages or actions delivered at the right moment have greater emotional and cognitive impact.

Why is Timing Essential?

Timing is effective because it is based on psychological principles that shape human behavior:

Psychological Rhythm

People have moments of greater emotional or intellectual vulnerability, and timing capitalizes on these rhythms.

Surprise Effect

Acting at the right moment can catch the other party off guard, enhancing the effectiveness of the action.

Synchronization with the Environment

External contexts, such as recent events or changes in the environment, create opportunities that can be exploited with precise timing.

Techniques for Applying Timing Strategically

Observe and Analyze the Context

Before acting, assess the emotional state, circumstances, and environment.

Example: Present an important idea during a meeting when the atmosphere is favorable and receptive.

Wait for a Moment of Vulnerability

Attack arguments or present solutions when the other party is uncertain or hesitant.

Example: During a negotiation, make your offer when the other party shows signs of doubt.

Use Strategic Pauses

In conversations, introduce pauses before saying something significant to create suspense and increase impact.

Align with Positive Emotions

Make requests or introduce ideas when the other party is in a positive emotional state.

Example: Wait until someone is excited about good news before proposing an idea that requires acceptance.

Adapt to External Events

Use external occurrences to reinforce your message or create opportunities.

Example: Mention a solution related to a recent problem affecting the interlocutor.

Act During Distraction

Present suggestions when the other party is busy or distracted, reducing their capacity for resistance.

Practical Applications of Timing

Negotiations
Wait until the other party shows signs of fatigue or is willing to end the discussion before presenting your proposal.

Marketing and Advertising
Launch products or campaigns at specific moments, such as holidays or significant events, to increase audience receptivity.

Interpersonal Relationships
Choosing the right moment to address delicate topics or make requests strengthens relationships and reduces conflict.

Leadership and Management
Introduce changes or directives when the team is motivated or open to new ideas.

Common Timing Mistakes and How to Avoid Them

Acting Too Early
Introducing an idea or proposal before the context is favorable can lead to unnecessary rejection.

Solution: Wait for clear signs of receptiveness before acting.

Delaying Too Long
Missing the ideal moment reduces the effectiveness of the action or message.

Solution: Stay attentive to the flow of events and be prepared to act quickly.

Ignoring Emotional Climate
Acting without considering the emotional state of the people involved can generate resistance or indifference.

Solution: Carefully evaluate the mood and reactions of others before acting.

Risks of Using Timing Strategically
Although timing is a powerful tool, it carries risks if not used correctly:

Perception of Manipulation

Using timing in an overtly calculated or obvious manner can generate distrust.

Negative Impact on Relationships

Poor timing may be perceived as insensitive or opportunistic.

Lack of Control

External factors, such as unexpected changes in the environment, can affect the success of timing.

Strategies to Resist Manipulative Timing

Just as you can use timing, others may apply it against you. To protect yourself:

Maintain Situational Awareness

Be alert to changes in the environment or in people's behavior around you.

Avoid Impulsive Reactions

Do not make important decisions immediately after an emotional or unexpected event.

Reevaluate Before Acting

When feeling pressured to respond quickly, ask for more time to assess the situation.

Exercises to Develop Timing

Practice in Everyday Conversations

Introduce important topics at specific moments and observe how people react.

Analyze Real Situations

Study events or interactions where timing was decisive to identify patterns and opportunities.

Simulate Timing Scenarios

Create hypothetical scenarios and practice deciding the ideal moment to act.

Ethics in Using Timing

Timing should be used responsibly to avoid unethical manipulation or exploiting vulnerabilities. Use it to:

Facilitate more productive and harmonious interactions.

Promote ideas or changes that benefit all parties.

Avoid unnecessary conflicts by addressing delicate issues at the right time.

Avoid:

Using timing to exploit negative emotions or vulnerabilities.

Manipulating situations in a calculated manner for purely personal gain.

The Connection to Dark Psychology

Timing exemplifies how dark psychology relies on observing and strategically controlling human dynamics. When used effectively, it allows you to influence almost imperceptibly, maximizing your chances of success in any interaction.

Mastering timing is more than knowing when to act—it is about understanding the natural flow of events and learning to navigate them with precision and intent.

Chapter 35
Creating Scarcity

Scarcity is one of the most powerful tools in dark psychology. Based on the principle that people value what appears rare or limited, creating scarcity can influence decisions, shape behaviors, and drive actions with remarkable effectiveness. This chapter explores the psychological foundations of scarcity, its strategic applications, and techniques for using it in a practical and ethical manner.

What is Scarcity?

Scarcity is a psychological phenomenon that occurs when something is perceived as limited in quantity, time, or access, automatically increasing its value or attractiveness. This principle is widely used in marketing, negotiations, leadership, and even personal interactions to motivate quick actions or reinforce the perception of exclusivity.

Why Does Scarcity Work?

The effectiveness of scarcity is rooted in fundamental human instincts and social norms:

Fear of Missing Out (FOMO)

The idea of losing something valuable or desirable creates urgency and drives quick decisions.

Perception of Value

The rarer something seems, the more it is valued, regardless of its actual worth.

Desire for Exclusivity

People tend to seek items, experiences, or opportunities that appear available to only a select few.

Competitive Behavior

Scarcity often triggers the desire to compete, making acquiring the item or advantage a symbol of status.

Forms of Scarcity

Time Scarcity

Limiting the availability of something to a specific period.
Example: "Offer valid only until midnight!"

Quantity Scarcity

Highlighting that only a few items or spots remain.
Example: "Only 3 units left in stock!"

Access Scarcity

Making something available only to a select group or by invitation.
Example: "Exclusive event for VIP members."

Information Scarcity

Creating value by restricting access to specific information.
Example: "Discover the secret that only a few people know!"

Techniques for Strategically Creating Scarcity

Set Clear Limits

Specify the limitation of time, quantity, or access to create urgency.
Example: "This opportunity is available only to the first 10 applicants."

Use Persuasive Language

Words like "rare," "exclusive," and "limited" reinforce the perception of scarcity.

Highlight Unique Benefits

Combine scarcity with the unique value of the offer to further increase its appeal.
Example: "This course won't be offered in this format again."

Introduce an Element of Competition

Emphasize that others are also interested, encouraging faster decisions.

Example: "Only two tickets left—secure yours before they're gone!"

Create a Context of Exclusivity

Restrict availability to make the item or opportunity seem more desirable.

Example: "Only selected customers have access to this special offer."

Practical Applications of Scarcity

Marketing and Sales

Promotional campaigns based on scarcity often result in higher conversion and engagement.

Example: Online stores display messages like "5 people are viewing this product now."

Negotiations

Highlighting time or resource limitations can pressure the other party to make decisions faster.

Example: "I can only hold this offer until the end of the day."

Personal Relationships

Creating a sense of limited time or attention can increase perceived value in relationships.

Example: "My schedule is packed this week, but we can meet at a specific time."

Professional Environment

Using scarcity of resources or opportunities can motivate teams or influence strategic decisions.

Example: "We only have capacity for one additional project this quarter."

Common Mistakes When Creating Scarcity and How to Avoid Them

Artificial or Unreal Scarcity

Exaggerating or inventing limitations can lead to mistrust when discovered.

Solution: Ensure limitations are real or clearly justified.

Overuse

Applying scarcity too frequently can reduce its effectiveness over time.

Solution: Use scarcity strategically during key moments.

Excessive Pressure

Forcing quick decisions may alienate people rather than persuade them.

Solution: Combine urgency with clear information and tangible benefits.

How to Resist Manipulative Scarcity

If you suspect scarcity is being used against you manipulatively, follow these strategies:

Question Validity

Investigate whether the presented limitation is real or just a persuasive tactic.

Analyze Actual Value

Ask yourself if the opportunity is worth the investment, regardless of its rarity.

Avoid Impulsive Reactions

Make decisions calmly, even under pressure of time or quantity.

Exercises to Practice Creating Scarcity

Develop Persuasive Messages

Create fictional advertisements or proposals that use scarcity and observe others' responses.

Test in Everyday Interactions

Introduce limitations in informal conversations and assess their impact on people's reactions.

Study Success Cases

Analyze marketing or sales campaigns that effectively employed scarcity.

Ethics in Creating Scarcity

Scarcity, when used ethically, can create value and encourage quicker decisions. However, it must be applied with transparency and responsibility. Use it to:

Highlight real and valuable opportunities.
Encourage actions that benefit all parties.
Increase the efficiency of processes or interactions.
Avoid:
Creating false or misleading limitations.
Using scarcity to manipulate critical or important decisions.

The Connection to Dark Psychology

The creation of scarcity illustrates how dark psychology can shape perceptions and subtly influence behaviors. This technique, when applied strategically, transforms how people perceive value and urgency, offering significant opportunities for influence in social, professional, and commercial interactions.

Mastering scarcity means understanding that value often lies not just in what is offered, but in the context in which it is presented.

Chapter 36
Behavior Modeling

Behavior modeling is a powerful technique that utilizes the observation and replication of actions, patterns, and characteristics of others to influence interactions and achieve goals. In dark psychology, this practice goes beyond mere imitation; it involves identifying effective behaviors in different contexts and strategically adapting them to create connections, establish authority, or shape others' perceptions. This chapter explores how to apply behavior modeling practically and ethically, highlighting its psychological foundations and strategies.

What Is Behavior Modeling?

Behavior modeling means observing the actions of a person or group and replicating them to achieve similar results. This technique is rooted in psychological theories such as Albert Bandura's social learning theory, which posits that people learn behaviors through observation and imitation.

In dark psychology, modeling is not limited to learning; it is used to create empathy, establish connections, and influence decisions by aligning with others' behaviors.

Why Does Modeling Work?

The effectiveness of behavior modeling is linked to universal psychological principles:

Instinctive Imitation

Humans have a natural tendency to imitate, especially in social contexts, to fit in with the group.

Similarity Effect

When people perceive similarities between themselves and others, they tend to trust more and feel more connected.

Social Norms

Observing and replicating successful behaviors aligns with the expectations and social norms of an environment.

Learning Through Observation

Behaviors observed in successful individuals are internalized as effective, encouraging replication.

Benefits of Behavior Modeling

Building Connections

Replicating subtle behavior patterns fosters empathy and strengthens relationships.

Adapting to New Environments

In unfamiliar contexts, modeling local behaviors facilitates integration.

Personal Improvement

Observing and applying practices of successful people helps develop positive skills and attitudes.

Social Influence

Adjusting your behavior to match others' can make you more persuasive and trustworthy.

Techniques for Behavior Modeling

Observe Subtle Details

Pay attention to speech patterns, gestures, and postures of individuals you wish to model.

Example: Notice how an effective leader maintains eye contact and adjusts their tone during meetings.

Match the Other Person's Rhythm

Synchronize your speaking speed, movements, or posture with the other person's to create a subconscious connection.

Example: If someone speaks calmly and slowly, adjust your pace to match theirs.

Imitate Effective Behaviors

Observe how successful people handle specific situations and practice these actions.

Example: Adopt negotiation techniques used by a successful colleague.

Mirror Body Language

Subtly replicate gestures, expressions, and postures to build empathy and strengthen rapport.

Example: If someone crosses their arms, wait a few seconds and discreetly do the same.

Identify Decision Patterns

Analyze how influential people make decisions and adjust your approach to reflect these patterns.

Enhance Observation Skills

Practice noticing details like microexpressions, tone of voice, and body language that reveal intentions and emotions.

Practical Examples of Behavior Modeling

In Professional Settings

Observe the behaviors of a respected colleague or leader and implement similar strategies to improve performance.

Example: Adopt the organizational and communication habits of a well-regarded manager.

In Negotiations

Adjust your tone and posture to match the other party's, establishing a connection and increasing receptivity.

In Personal Relationships

Model active listening and empathy behaviors demonstrated by emotionally intelligent individuals to improve interpersonal connections.

For Personal Development

Study the routines and habits of successful individuals and adapt these practices to your life.

Example: Incorporate the morning routines of leaders you admire.

Common Mistakes in Behavior Modeling and How to Avoid Them

Overdoing Imitation

Overtly replicating behaviors can appear forced or artificial.

Solution: Be subtle when mirroring gestures or speech patterns.

Focusing on Ineffective Behaviors

Not all observed behaviors are useful or appropriate for every context.

Solution: Select behaviors aligned with your goals.

Ignoring Your Own Identity

Adopting behaviors inconsistent with your personality can seem inauthentic.

Solution: Customize observed practices to suit your style.

Neglecting Different Contexts

Behaviors effective in one setting may not work in another.

Solution: Adapt to the context and adjust your approach as needed.

Exercises for Practicing Behavior Modeling

Video Analysis

Watch interviews or lectures by influential individuals and identify specific behaviors you can model.

Mirroring in Conversations

Practice subtly mirroring body language and speech patterns during daily interactions.

Role-Playing with Friends

Simulate scenarios where you replicate successful behaviors in specific situations, such as negotiations or presentations.

Observation Diary

Record behaviors you observe in successful individuals and note how they could be applied to your life.

Ethics in Behavior Modeling

Behavior modeling should be used responsibly, respecting the boundaries and authenticity of interactions. Use it to:

Learn from the best and continuously improve yourself.

Build authentic connections through empathy and adaptation.

Resolve conflicts or create consensus in complex interactions.

Avoid:

Using modeled behaviors to manipulate or exploit vulnerabilities.

Adopting practices that compromise your integrity or values.

Connection to Dark Psychology

Behavior modeling is a sophisticated technique that demonstrates how observation and adaptation can significantly enhance your influence and effectiveness. When used strategically, it enables you to adapt to different scenarios, establish deeper connections, and achieve goals with greater precision.

Mastering behavior modeling goes beyond imitation—it is about understanding the foundations of success and integrating them into your style to shape a future of impact and relevance.

Chapter 37
Introduction to Conversational Hypnosis

Conversational hypnosis is an advanced influence technique that uses language patterns and psychological strategies to access a person's subconscious, facilitating the acceptance of ideas or suggestions. Unlike traditional hypnosis, it does not require a deep trance state; it occurs in everyday interactions, often without the interlocutor's awareness. This chapter explores the fundamentals of conversational hypnosis, its psychological foundations, and practical methods for applying it strategically and ethically.

What Is Conversational Hypnosis?

Conversational hypnosis is the ability to influence thoughts, emotions, and behaviors through subtle and directed communication. It combines elements of psychology, language, and persuasion to create a subconscious connection, leading the listener to accept ideas or act according to suggestions.

The technique is based on:

Focus and Suggestion

Using speech patterns to capture attention and introduce suggestions non-intrusively.

Rapport

Building a relationship of empathy and trust to facilitate message acceptance.

Accessing the Subconscious

Guiding the interlocutor's attention to a receptive mental state, reducing conscious barriers.

Why Does Conversational Hypnosis Work?

Its effectiveness is rooted in fundamental principles of psychology:

Focused Attention States

By capturing attention, it is possible to direct the mind's focus to specific ideas, making them more influential.

Natural Suggestibility

The human brain is naturally receptive to suggestions, especially in states of relaxation or concentration.

Reduced Resistance

The subtle approach of conversational hypnosis bypasses conscious barriers, avoiding active resistance.

Emotional Connection

Creating empathy and rapport establishes an emotional foundation that reinforces message acceptance.

Fundamental Elements of Conversational Hypnosis

Hypnotic Language

Using carefully chosen words and phrases to induce states of suggestibility.

Patterns of Rhythm and Tone

Speech rhythm and tone play a critical role in creating a relaxing and receptive environment.

Stories and Metaphors

Engaging narratives help access the subconscious, conveying ideas indirectly and effectively.

Embedded Suggestions

Inserting commands or messages within seemingly neutral sentences.

Example: "You can start to feel more relaxed as you listen to my words."

Strategic Pauses and Silence

Moments of pause give the listener time to internalize the messages.

Practical Techniques of Conversational Hypnosis

Build Initial Rapport

Establish empathy through mirrored body language, a similar tone of voice, and genuine interest.

Use Open-Ended Questions

Questions that encourage reflection help guide the interlocutor's thoughts.

Example: "How do you think this could improve your life?"

Employ Ambiguous Phrases

Words with multiple meanings keep the listener engaged while the subconscious processes the message.

Example: "You can begin to notice something important from now on."

Embed Commands

Insert direct suggestions within longer sentences to reduce resistance.

Example: "While you consider your options, choose the best one for yourself."

Lead with Metaphors

Use stories or comparisons to convey messages indirectly.

Example: "This is like planting a seed; over time, it grows into something meaningful."

Redirect Attention

Shift focus from the conscious mind to create openness in the subconscious.

Example: "As you focus on how this idea works, you may begin to relax."

Applications of Conversational Hypnosis

Negotiations

Influence decisions by creating an atmosphere of trust and reducing resistance to proposals.

Teaching and Training

Use hypnotic language to reinforce learning and engagement in students or team members.

Marketing and Sales

Redirect attention to the benefits of products or services, facilitating acceptance.

Personal Relationships
Improve communication and build deeper connections through empathetic narratives and suggestions.

Self-Improvement
Apply the technique to reinforce positive messages and achieve personal or professional goals.

Risks and Limitations of Conversational Hypnosis
Although a powerful tool, conversational hypnosis has limitations and risks that must be considered:

Conscious Resistance
People with strong skepticism may reject suggestions if they detect an influence attempt.

Perception of Manipulation
If used overtly or unethically, it can damage relationships and generate mistrust.

Ethical Limitations
Using the technique to exploit or manipulate vulnerabilities can have negative consequences for both parties.

How to Resist Conversational Hypnosis

Stay Conscious
Pay attention to the language and tone used in important interactions.

Question Suggestions
Critically evaluate commands or messages to identify possible influence attempts.

Strengthen Mental Barriers
Focus on your objectives and values to avoid being swayed by external suggestions.

Exercises for Practicing Conversational Hypnosis

Develop Persuasive Stories
Practice creating narratives that incorporate embedded suggestions and meaningful metaphors.

Experiment with Tone and Rhythm
Record your voice, adjusting rhythm and intonation to evoke different emotional states.

Apply in Daily Interactions
Introduce subtle suggestions in informal conversations and observe the reactions.

Study Real Cases
Analyze speeches, marketing campaigns, or influential leaders who use conversational hypnosis.

Ethics in Conversational Hypnosis
As with any dark psychology technique, conversational hypnosis must be used responsibly. Use it to:

Promote positive solutions in negotiations or conflicts.
Foster genuine engagement and trust in social interactions.
Help others overcome barriers or achieve important goals.
Avoid:
Exploiting vulnerabilities for selfish gains.
Inducing actions contrary to the interlocutor's values or interests.

Connection to Dark Psychology
Conversational hypnosis demonstrates how the power of language and psychology can be used to subtly and effectively influence. When applied strategically, it transforms ordinary interactions into opportunities for connection, persuasion, and mutual growth.

Mastering this technique is learning to touch the subconscious mind with precision, understanding that words not only communicate but also shape perceptions and realities.

Chapter 38
Advanced Emotional Control

Advanced emotional control is the ability to strategically manage your emotions in high-pressure situations, as well as influence the emotions of others to achieve your goals. In the realm of dark psychology, this skill is essential for maintaining control in challenging interactions, projecting authority, and creating a lasting emotional impact. This chapter explores the most effective emotional control techniques, highlighting their practical application and ethical importance.

What is Advanced Emotional Control?

Advanced emotional control goes beyond merely suppressing emotional reactions. It involves:

Emotional Self-Awareness

Recognizing and understanding your emotions in real time.

Intentional Regulation

Modifying or adjusting emotions to align with your goals.

External Influence

Identifying and subtly manipulating others' emotions to achieve desired outcomes.

This skill is particularly useful in conflict situations, negotiations, leadership, and personal interactions, where emotions often play a central role in decisions and behaviors.

Why is Emotional Control Essential?

Reducing Impulsive Reactions

Uncontrolled emotions can lead to hasty decisions or damage your image.

Building Trust
Demonstrating emotional stability inspires confidence in both personal and professional environments.

Maintaining Control
Managing your emotions allows you to remain in control during tense or unpredictable situations.

Facilitating Influence
Understanding others' emotions enables you to steer them toward behaviors that align with your objectives.

Fundamental Principles of Advanced Emotional Control

Self-Awareness
Understand your emotions and the triggers that provoke them.

Example: Realizing you tend to feel frustrated in intense meetings helps you prepare to respond calmly.

Cognitive Reframing
Reinterpret emotionally challenging situations in a more neutral or positive light.

Example: Viewing criticism as a learning opportunity rather than a personal attack.

Strategic Detachment
Emotionally distance yourself from a situation to evaluate the best possible response.

Emotional Anchoring
Use positive memories or thoughts to stabilize your emotional state during difficult moments.

Manipulating Others' Emotions
Identify others' emotional states and adjust your approach to influence them effectively.

Example: Using a calming tone to disarm someone who is upset.

Advanced Emotional Control Techniques

Conscious Breathing
Breathing techniques can immediately reduce the impact of intense emotions.

Example: Inhale for four seconds, hold for four, and exhale for four to stabilize your nervous system.

Positive Self-Talk

Replace negative or automatic thoughts with encouraging and rational messages.

Example: "I am in control of this situation and can handle it effectively."

Response Delay

Pause before reacting emotionally, giving yourself time to process the situation logically.

Example: Counting to ten before responding to a provocative comment.

Immersion in Present Sensations

Focus on physical details of the present moment to ground yourself in reality.

Example: Paying attention to the texture of an object in your hand or the sensation of air on your skin.

Emotional Mirroring

Align your emotions with another person's state to build rapport and then guide the interaction toward a more positive emotion.

Example: Initially showing empathy to someone frustrated and gradually calming them with a reassuring tone.

Meditation and Mindfulness Practice

Develop the ability to observe and accept emotions without reacting automatically.

Practical Applications of Advanced Emotional Control

Negotiations

Staying calm during tough negotiations enhances your ability to argue logically and spot opportunities.

Leadership

Leaders who demonstrate emotional stability inspire trust and help maintain team morale during crises.

Personal Relationships

Managing your emotions in personal conflicts strengthens relationships and prevents unnecessary escalation.

Crisis Management

Emotional control enables rational decision-making under pressure, even in high-intensity situations.

Common Mistakes and How to Avoid Them

Suppressing Emotions

Ignoring or suppressing emotions can lead to unexpected outbursts.

Solution: Acknowledge emotions and deal with them healthily.

Focusing Only on Yourself

Neglecting others' emotions can limit your effectiveness in influencing them.

Solution: Pay attention to others' emotional reactions and adjust your approach.

False Neutrality

Appearing emotionless can be interpreted as coldness or indifference.

Solution: Show controlled emotions genuinely to build trust.

How to Identify Others' Emotional States

Observe Nonverbal Cues

Pay attention to body language, facial expressions, and tone of voice.

Listen Beyond Words

Focus on the underlying emotions conveyed in what is being said.

Ask Reflective Questions

Open-ended questions can reveal more about someone's emotional state.

Example: "How do you feel about this?"

Identify Patterns

Recognize recurring emotional triggers in specific people to predict their reactions.

Exercises to Practice Advanced Emotional Control

Emotion Journal

Record your emotions daily, identifying triggers and recurring patterns.

High-Pressure Simulations

Practice responding to challenging scenarios in a controlled environment, such as roleplays with colleagues or friends.

Breathing Exercises

Dedicate a few minutes daily to conscious breathing practices to enhance emotional resilience.

Observer Feedback

Ask friends or colleagues to observe how you manage emotions in interactions and provide feedback.

Ethics in Advanced Emotional Control

Using emotional control to influence others requires responsibility. Use it to:

Resolve conflicts constructively.

Inspire trust and stability in teams or groups.

Protect yourself from harmful emotional manipulation.

Avoid:

Exploiting emotional vulnerabilities for personal gain.

Manipulating others' emotions in ways that cause harm or distress.

Connection with Dark Psychology

Advanced emotional control exemplifies how dark psychology empowers individuals to navigate challenging situations with clarity and influence. By mastering your emotions and understanding those of others, you position yourself as a force of impact in any interaction.

Mastering this skill is not just about internal control—it's about creating a balance between rationality and emotion, shaping the world around you with precision and purpose.

Chapter 39
Dealing with Criticism

Knowing how to handle criticism is an essential skill for protecting your emotional integrity and strengthening your position in social and professional interactions. In the realm of dark psychology, dealing with criticism does not merely mean accepting or rejecting feedback but also using it as a strategic tool to deflect attacks, consolidate your image, and, in some cases, manipulate others' perceptions to your advantage. This chapter addresses how to interpret, react to, and respond to criticism strategically and effectively while preserving your confidence and influence.

What is Criticism?

Criticism consists of evaluations, often negative, regarding behaviors, ideas, or actions. It can be:

Constructive

Provides feedback aimed at helping you improve.

Example: "I think you can enhance your presentation by adjusting the tone for a more technical audience."

Destructive

Aims to hurt, demotivate, or criticize without offering solutions.

Example: "You always make mistakes in your presentations."

Veiled

Disguised as compliments but carrying underlying criticism.

Example: "Your work is great, considering you had so little time to prepare."

Why Does Criticism Have Such an Impact?

Criticism has a significant emotional impact because it touches on self-esteem, the desire for social acceptance, and the fear of failure. This effect can be intensified by:

Fear of Rejection
Criticism may be perceived as a threat to social connection.

Excessive Self-Criticism
People prone to blaming themselves may internalize criticism more deeply.

Cognitive Dissonance
When criticism contradicts your self-perception, it can cause psychological discomfort.

Strategies for Dealing with Criticism

Effectively dealing with criticism involves more than reacting—it requires analysis, strategy, and emotional control.

Evaluate the Intention
Determine whether the criticism is constructive, destructive, or veiled.

Constructive: Consider how to use it for growth.

Destructive: Neutralize it without being affected.

Control Your Emotional Reaction
Avoid impulsive or angry responses. Take a deep breath, count to ten, and respond calmly.

Acknowledge the Feedback
Show maturity and disarm criticism by recognizing it, even if you disagree.

Example: "Thank you for sharing your opinion; I'll take that into consideration."

Request Clarification
Asking for specific details disarms vague or malicious criticism.

Example: "Could you elaborate on what exactly you think could be improved?"

Redirect the Conversation

Use criticism as a starting point to highlight your achievements or reaffirm your competence.

Example: "I understand your point. That said, the final results met expectations, didn't they?"

Reframe the Criticism

Turn negative criticism into opportunities for learning or positive affirmations about your actions.

Example: "Yes, it was challenging, but I learned a lot from the experience."

Set Boundaries

For destructive criticism, firmly establish that certain comments are unacceptable.

Example: "I appreciate feedback, but I prefer it to be presented constructively."

Techniques for Defending Against Malicious Criticism

Disarm the Critic

Respond calmly and maturely, discouraging further attacks.

Use Humor

A well-humored response can neutralize aggressive criticism.

Example: "You really excel at finding my weak points, don't you?"

Ignore When Necessary

In some cases, the best response is no attention at all, which can discourage the critic.

Confront Directly

For persistent or destructive criticism, address the issue assertively and respectfully.

Example: "I'd like to understand if there's something specific we need to resolve between us."

How to Use Criticism to Your Advantage

Criticism, when well managed, can be transformed into opportunities to strengthen your image and improve your skills:

Identify Areas for Improvement
Even destructive criticism may contain valuable insights into blind spots.

Demonstrate Resilience
Responding to criticism with composure and professionalism increases your credibility.

Build Your Narrative
Use criticism to reaffirm your competence and proactivity.
Example: "I received feedback on this and am already implementing improvements."

Strengthen Relationships
Showing openness to feedback can improve interpersonal and professional connections.

Risks and Precautions When Dealing with Criticism

Over-Defensiveness
Excessive defenses can make you appear insecure or unprepared.

Internalizing Negative Criticism
Allowing destructive criticism to affect your self-esteem can undermine your confidence.

Avoiding Necessary Conflicts
Ignoring criticism when a response is needed may be interpreted as weakness.

Exercises for Practicing Criticism Management

Feedback Journal
Record criticisms you've received, analyze your reactions, and identify areas for improvement.

Simulations with Colleagues
Practice responding to criticism in hypothetical scenarios with friends or colleagues.

Reinterpretation of Past Criticisms
Review old criticisms and try to identify lessons or useful patterns for your development.

Observation Study
Observe how leaders or public figures handle criticism and adapt techniques that work for you.

Ethics in Dealing with Criticism

Responding to criticism ethically strengthens your integrity and protects your relationships:

Use criticism as opportunities for learning and growth.

Respond respectfully, even in difficult situations.

Avoid using criticism to humiliate or harm others.

Connection with Dark Psychology

Dealing with criticism is a central aspect of dark psychology because it involves both emotional control and the ability to manipulate perceptions in challenging situations. Turning criticism into opportunities is a sign of psychological and social mastery.

Mastering this skill is not only about self-protection—it's about growing through adversity, strengthening your position, and building a reputation for resilience and effectiveness.

Chapter 40
Using Rewards

The strategic use of rewards is a powerful tool for influencing behaviors and shaping relationships. Rewards, when applied correctly, encourage cooperation, build bonds, and guide actions without the need for confrontations or impositions. In the realm of dark psychology, they are used to foster loyalty, reinforce desired attitudes, and even create emotional or intellectual dependence in a subtle manner. This chapter explores the psychological foundations of rewards, their strategic applications, and how to use them practically and ethically.

What Are Rewards?

Rewards are positive stimuli given after a desired behavior, increasing the likelihood of that behavior being repeated in the future. They can be tangible or intangible, varying in form and impact depending on the context.

Types of Rewards

Tangible Rewards

Physical objects or benefits that have perceived value.

Example: Money, gifts, discounts.

Intangible Rewards

Emotional or social benefits without direct material value.

Example: Praise, recognition, attention.

Contingent Rewards

Offered directly in response to a specific action.

Example: "If you achieve this goal, you'll receive a bonus."

Intermittent Rewards

Offered randomly or occasionally, generating constant anticipation.

Example: Surprise prizes for engaged participants.

Why Do Rewards Work?

The effectiveness of rewards is rooted in psychological principles governing human behavior:

Operant Conditioning

Developed by B.F. Skinner, this concept shows that positively reinforced behaviors are more likely to be repeated.

Dopamine Release

Rewards activate the brain's reward system, releasing dopamine and creating a pleasurable association with the behavior.

Increased Motivation

Knowing a reward awaits reinforces effort and commitment toward achieving the goal.

Expectation Creation

Intermittent rewards foster anticipation and continuous engagement.

How to Use Rewards Strategically

Define Desired Behaviors

Clearly identify the behavior you wish to reinforce before introducing a reward.

Choose Appropriate Rewards

Ensure the reward is relevant and valued by the person or group.

Example: For a coworker, public recognition might be more valuable than a material gift.

Set Clear Rules

Establish specific conditions for earning the reward, avoiding misunderstandings or feelings of unfairness.

Example: "You'll receive the benefit after three consecutive months of above-average performance."

Use Intermittent Rewards

Offer rewards randomly to maintain interest and constant engagement.

Incorporate Social Rewards

Rewards like compliments, gratitude, or gestures of appreciation are effective, especially in personal contexts.

Combine Tangible and Intangible Rewards

Mix material and emotional incentives for a more comprehensive impact.

Practical Examples of Reward Use

In the Workplace

Use rewards to encourage productivity and engagement.

Example: Publicly recognize an employee who exceeded expectations, paired with a bonus.

In Personal Relationships

Offer emotional rewards, such as extra attention or words of affirmation, to reinforce desired behaviors.

Example: "I loved how you handled that situation. You really did a great job."

In Education

Motivate students with rewards that recognize effort and progress.

Example: "If you complete all the week's assignments, we'll have a special activity on Friday."

In Sales and Marketing

Rewards create loyalty and increase conversion chances.

Example: Offer an exclusive discount for customers who complete a satisfaction survey.

Risks and Limitations of Using Rewards

While effective, the use of rewards requires balance and caution:

Dependency on Rewards

Overuse can lead to dependence, where behaviors occur only in anticipation of an incentive.

Solution: Combine rewards with intrinsic motivators, such as purpose or meaning.

Perception of Manipulation
Rewards may be seen as a calculated attempt at control.
Solution: Be transparent and genuine when offering them.

Diminished Impact
Frequent rewards lose their value over time.
Solution: Vary the type and frequency of rewards.

Perceived Injustice
Unequal distribution of rewards can lead to resentment.
Solution: Ensure criteria are clear and fair.

How to Resist Manipulative Use of Rewards Against You

Just as you can use rewards to influence others, it's important to recognize when they're being used manipulatively:

Question Intentions
Analyze whether the offered reward seeks to encourage behavior contrary to your values or interests.

Evaluate Cost-Benefit
Assess whether the effort or concession required to achieve the reward is worthwhile.

Differentiate Rewards from Pressure
Ensure the reward is genuine and not a guise for coercion.

Exercises to Practice Using Rewards

Develop a Reward Plan
Create a reward scheme for a specific situation, such as motivating a team or improving a relationship.

Observe Rewards in Action
Analyze marketing campaigns or incentive systems to identify how rewards are used strategically.

Practice Positive Feedback
Incorporate praise and recognition into daily interactions, observing people's reactions.

Ethics in Using Rewards

While rewards are a powerful tool, their use must be guided by ethics and responsibility. Use them to:

Promote growth and development.
Reinforce behaviors benefiting all parties involved.
Build stronger connections based on genuine recognition.

Avoid:

Using rewards to manipulate or exploit vulnerabilities.

Making promises of rewards you cannot or do not intend to fulfill.

The Connection with Dark Psychology

The strategic use of rewards exemplifies how small gestures can have a significant impact on behaviors and attitudes. When applied intelligently, they become a subtle and effective tool for guiding interactions and achieving objectives.

Mastering this technique involves understanding that true influence lies not only in what you offer but also in how you present and structure those offerings, creating an environment where people choose to align with your intentions.

Chapter 41
Narrative Control

Narrative control is a sophisticated influence technique that uses the construction and manipulation of stories to shape perceptions and behaviors. Whether in social, professional, or media contexts, those who control the narrative wield power over how events are interpreted and what actions are taken as a result of those interpretations. This chapter explores how to structure, direct, and strategically use narratives to influence public or private perceptions, creating favorable and impactful outcomes.

What Is Narrative Control?

Narrative control refers to the ability to shape the dominant story surrounding events, people, or situations. It involves selecting which facts to emphasize, how to present them, and what emotions or messages to convey.

An effective narrative:

Emotionally connects with the audience.

Simplifies complexity to make it understandable.

Directs attention to elements that align with desired objectives.

Why Is Narrative Control Powerful?

Narratives shape how people perceive reality. The power of this technique lies in:

Emotional Power

Stories activate emotions, making people more receptive and engaged.

Ease of Memorization

A well-structured narrative is easier to remember than isolated facts.

Influence on Decision-Makers

Narratives shape how problems are understood and what solutions appear most appropriate.

Consensus Building

They provide a unifying perspective, especially in polarized environments.

Key Elements of a Strategic Narrative

Central Character

This can be a hero, villain, or victim. Readers or listeners connect emotionally with them.

Example: In a company, the customer can be portrayed as the hero of a campaign.

Conflict

The narrative needs a challenge or problem to emotionally engage the audience.

Resolution

Provide a clear solution that aligns the story with your objectives.

Central Message

Ensure the narrative reinforces the main idea you want to communicate.

Tone and Style

Choose a tone that resonates with the target audience—optimistic, dramatic, inspiring, or persuasive.

Techniques for Strategic Narrative Control

Set the Agenda

Be the first to present the narrative. Whoever defines the initial context often shapes the rest of the discourse.

Example: A company in crisis publicly taking responsibility can better control the impact on public opinion.

Use Powerful Language

Select words and phrases that evoke emotions and resonate with the audience.

Example: Instead of "problem," use "challenge" to create a more positive perception.

Simplify Complexity

Summarize complex issues in a clear and accessible way. Confusing narratives lose effectiveness.

Include Examples and Metaphors

Use real stories or analogies to reinforce your narrative and make it memorable.

Redirect Unwanted Focus

If there are unfavorable elements in the narrative, shift attention to more positive aspects.

Example: In response to criticism of a product, emphasize future improvements and commitments to quality.

Integrate into Existing Narratives

Link your narrative to ideas or stories already accepted by the audience to increase credibility.

Applications of Narrative Control

In the Workplace

Use narratives to present projects, motivate teams, or manage internal crises.

Example: Frame a restructuring as an opportunity for growth and innovation.

In Personal Relationships

Craft narratives that explain actions or decisions in ways that generate understanding and empathy.

Example: When justifying a career change, create a story that highlights your values and ambitions.

In Marketing Campaigns

Connect products or services to inspiring stories that emotionally resonate with the audience.

In Politics and Leadership

Control narratives to shape public perception of events or policies, building consensus or support.

Risks of Narrative Control and How to Avoid Them

Exaggeration or Excessive Manipulation

Overly artificial or manipulative narratives can breed distrust.

Solution: Base your stories on truths or verifiable facts.

Conflict with Other Narratives

If your narrative contradicts a widely accepted story, you may face resistance.

Solution: Acknowledge and integrate elements of the existing narrative to create a smooth transition.

Lack of Clarity

Confusing or overly detailed narratives lose impact.

Solution: Keep it simple and focus on a clear central message.

How to Identify and Respond to Hostile Narratives

Identify Intentions

Determine the objective of the hostile narrative and who benefits from it.

Counter with Facts

Present clear evidence that contradicts unfavorable elements of the narrative.

Reframe the Story

Replace the hostile narrative with a version that aligns with your perspective.

Example: Reframe criticism as demonstrations of interest or commitment to improvement.

Exercises to Practice Narrative Control

Story Creation

Develop narratives for common events, such as explaining a delay or presenting an idea.

Analyze Public Narratives

Study how leaders, companies, or media shape narratives around recent events.

Simulations

Practice responding to fictional scenarios with narratives that redirect criticism or shape perceptions.

Ethics in Narrative Control

Narrative control is a powerful tool and must be used ethically and responsibly. Use it to:

Promote understanding and collaboration.
Resolve conflicts constructively.
Inspire positive changes in individuals or groups.
Avoid:
Manipulating facts to deceive or exploit.
Using narratives to misinform or cause harm.

The Connection with Dark Psychology

Controlling narratives is a clear manifestation of psychological power in action. Those who master this skill can transform perceptions, build alliances, and shape realities.

Mastering narrative control is not just about telling stories but about understanding how people interpret and react to them, influencing the course of events with precision and purpose.

Chapter 42
Advanced Social Manipulation

Advanced social manipulation is a technique that uses complex psychological strategies to influence groups or individuals on deeper and more subtle levels. Unlike simpler approaches to manipulation, this method focuses on scenario building, the creation of strategic alliances, and the use of social dynamics to achieve specific objectives. This chapter explores advanced tactics, their psychological foundations, and practical applications, highlighting how these techniques can be employed effectively and ethically.

What Is Advanced Social Manipulation?

Advanced social manipulation is the ability to influence collective or individual behavior through meticulous strategies that exploit needs, emotions, and power dynamics.

These tactics go beyond individual interactions, affecting:

Group Dynamics

Creating alliances, influencing opinions, and shaping behaviors in social or organizational contexts.

Perception Patterns

Shaping how a group perceives an event, idea, or individual.

Collective Behaviors

Directing group action toward a specific goal.

Why Does Advanced Social Manipulation Work?

Its effectiveness lies in understanding and leveraging fundamental factors that govern social behavior:

Need for Belonging

People seek acceptance and approval within social groups.

Social Pressure

The desire for conformity can lead individuals to adopt behaviors they wouldn't otherwise.

Natural Hierarchies

Groups tend to form power and influence hierarchies, which can be exploited to direct actions.

Emotional Factors

Shared emotions, such as fear, enthusiasm, or outrage, influence collective decisions.

Techniques for Advanced Social Manipulation

1. Divide and Conquer

Identify divisions within a group and amplify them to fragment unity and direct actions.

Example: Highlight conflicting interests among subgroups to create opportunities for influence.

2. Creation of Strategic Alliances

Form partnerships with influential individuals within the group to legitimize your ideas or actions.

Example: In a corporate environment, seek support from team leaders to promote your agenda.

3. Manipulation of Social Norms

Introduce or reinforce norms that align with your goals.

Example: In a new project, establish a behavior that benefits your position as the "standard."

4. Redefinition of Collective Narratives

Control the dominant narrative within a group to shape perceptions and align behaviors.

Example: Frame a crisis as an opportunity for unity under your leadership.

5. Use of Subliminal Messaging

Introduce ideas or suggestions indirectly to influence collective thinking.

6. Creation of Perceived Scarcity in the Group

Make the group believe that a resource or opportunity is limited, prompting immediate action.

How to Apply Advanced Social Manipulation Strategically

1. Analyze Group Dynamics

Before acting, identify formal and informal leaders, subgroups, and potential sources of conflict.

2. Build a Trustworthy Image

Position yourself as reliable and indispensable to gain influence without raising suspicion.

3. Introduce Changes Gradually

Abrupt changes can generate resistance; implement new ideas or behaviors incrementally.

4. Activate Collective Emotions

Use emotions like fear or enthusiasm to mobilize the group toward a goal.

5. Reinforce Desired Behaviors

Publicly recognize and reward actions aligned with your objectives.

6. Leverage the Power of Example

Demonstrate behaviors you want the group to emulate, presenting them as normal or desirable.

Practical Applications of Advanced Social Manipulation

Organizational Leadership

Shape the culture of a team or organization to align with strategic goals.

Politics and Activism

Influence social or political groups by presenting ideas that connect with collective emotions.

Marketing and Advertising

Design campaigns that leverage social dynamics to drive engagement and conversions.

Conflict Resolution

Redirect the focus of conflicting groups toward a common goal, minimizing divisions.

Common Mistakes in Advanced Social Manipulation

Underestimating Group Dynamics

Ignoring alliances or internal conflicts can result in unexpected resistance.

Solution: Observe carefully before taking action.

Over-Controlling

Attempting to manipulate all aspects of a group may lead to distrust and rebellion.

Solution: Be selective in your actions and maintain subtlety.

Lack of Planning

Impulsive actions without a clear plan can backfire.

Solution: Develop detailed strategies beforehand.

Neglecting Ethics

Manipulations perceived as unethical can damage credibility.

Solution: Use these techniques to achieve legitimate goals and avoid harm.

How to Identify Social Manipulation Targeting You

Notice Changes in Group Dynamics

Someone may be creating divisions or shaping norms for personal benefit.

Question Dominant Narratives

Assess whether the presented narrative aligns with reality or benefits a specific individual.

Be Wary of Heightened Emotions

Check if a group is being emotionally manipulated into making rash decisions.

Recognize False Allies

Identify individuals who appear to support your ideas but may serve other interests.

Exercises to Practice Advanced Social Manipulation

Group Analysis

Examine the dynamics of social or professional groups you are part of, identifying leaders and subgroups.

Plan Strategic Interventions

Create hypothetical scenarios and develop social manipulation strategies to achieve specific goals.

Apply Techniques in Small Groups

Practice subtle social manipulation in low-stakes contexts, such as with friends or small projects.

Observe Effective Leaders

Study how successful leaders use social manipulation techniques to achieve results.

Ethics in Advanced Social Manipulation

As with any powerful tool, these techniques must be used responsibly. Utilize them to:

Resolve conflicts constructively.

Mobilize groups toward positive and aligned goals.

Influence without exploiting or harming others.

Avoid:

Dividing groups for selfish gain.

Emotional manipulation for unfair advantage.

Connection to Dark Psychology

Advanced social manipulation synthesizes skills developed in earlier chapters. Here, individual techniques converge to influence groups strategically and subtly. When used carefully and purposefully, it transforms complex interactions into opportunities for significant impact.

Mastering this skill is an essential step for those seeking to shape social dynamics and achieve results that transcend the individual, consolidating influence and leadership.

Chapter 43
Protecting Yourself from Manipulation

While dark psychology provides powerful tools to influence and shape behavior, it is equally important to understand how to protect yourself from manipulative tactics directed at you. This chapter explores practical strategies to recognize, resist, and neutralize manipulation attempts in various contexts, strengthening your psychological and emotional autonomy.

What Is Manipulation?

Manipulation is the act of influencing another person's actions, thoughts, or emotions in a subtle or deceptive way, often serving interests that are not apparent to the manipulated individual. Although not all manipulation is negative, the risk of exploitation makes protection essential.

Common Types of Manipulation

1. Emotional Manipulation

Exploits emotions like guilt, fear, or empathy to control behavior.

Example: "If you really cared about me, you'd do this."

2. Gaslighting

Causes someone to question their perception of reality.

Example: "You're overreacting; that never happened."

3. Use of Rewards and Punishments

Offers incentives or threatens consequences to force decisions.

Example: "If you do this, you'll get a raise; if not, forget about the promotion."

4. Appeal to Authority

Uses status or power to invalidate arguments or impose ideas.

Example: "I know what's best because I have more experience."

5. Isolation

Attempts to separate the person from their support networks to increase control.

Example: "Those people don't really understand you."

6. Subtle Persuasion

Uses indirect suggestions to plant ideas or induce behaviors.

Example: "It would be great if someone could handle this... but no one here seems capable."

Why Are We Vulnerable to Manipulation?

Manipulation exploits natural human vulnerabilities, such as:

Need for Acceptance

The desire to be loved or accepted can lead to compromises.

Excessive Trust

Blind trust in close relationships can open the door to manipulation.

Fear of Conflict

Avoiding confrontation can make it easier to give in to manipulation.

Lack of Self-Awareness

Not understanding your own emotions or limits makes it easier for others to control you.

How to Recognize Signs of Manipulation

Feelings of Guilt or Constant Pressure

If you frequently feel guilty or pressured, you may be under manipulation.

Cognitive Dissonance

When your actions don't reflect your values or beliefs, external influence may be at play.

Ambiguity or Inconsistency

Manipulators often change narratives or avoid clear explanations.

Loss of Control

If someone else always seems to dictate conditions or decisions, it could indicate manipulation.

Gradual Isolation

Notice if you're drifting away from friends or family without clear reasons.

Strategies to Protect Yourself from Manipulation

1. Strengthen Your Self-Awareness

Understand your emotions, values, and boundaries. People who know themselves well are less likely to succumb to manipulation.

2. Question Intentions

Always ask why someone is requesting or suggesting something.

Example: "Why is this so important to you?"

3. Maintain Emotional Control

Manipulators often exploit intense emotions. Take a deep breath and assess the situation calmly.

4. Set Clear Boundaries

Don't hesitate to say "no" or decline something that goes against your interests or values.

5. Seek External Perspectives

Talk to trusted people about suspicious situations to gain alternative viewpoints.

6. Document Interactions

Record relevant conversations or events, especially in professional environments.

7. Practice Delayed Responses

Don't feel pressured to make immediate decisions. Ask for time to think.

Example: "I need a moment to consider this."

Techniques to Neutralize Manipulation

1. Confront Assertively

Expose manipulation in a direct and respectful way.

Example: "It seems like you're trying to make me feel guilty to agree with this. Let's discuss the issue objectively."

2. Redirect the Conversation

Shift focus to disarm the manipulation attempt.

Example: "I understand what you want, but can we discuss how this impacts everyone involved?"

3. Use Specific Questions

Pointed questions can uncover the logic or hidden intentions of the manipulator.

Example: "Why do you believe this is the only solution?"

4. Stand Firm in Your Values

Reaffirm your beliefs and priorities, even under pressure.

5. Involve a Third Party

Bring in a mediator or witness in situations where manipulation is frequent.

Exercises to Improve Resistance to Manipulation

Scenario Analysis

Reflect on past interactions to identify possible manipulation scenarios.

Simulations with Friends or Colleagues

Practice confronting manipulation in fictitious scenarios to build confidence.

Meditation and Mindfulness

Develop emotional self-awareness to recognize manipulation in real-time.

Study Manipulative Behaviors

Learn about manipulation techniques to identify them more easily.

How to Build Psychological Resilience

Strengthen Your Support Network

Maintain relationships with trustworthy people who can offer support in moments of doubt.

Establish Clear Priorities

Knowing what's most important to you reduces the likelihood of succumbing to external pressures.

Practice Emotional Self-Sufficiency

Reduce dependence on external validation, making you less vulnerable to emotional manipulation.

Ethics in Protecting Against Manipulation

Protecting yourself from manipulation doesn't mean creating unnecessary conflict or adopting an excessively defensive stance. Use these strategies to:

Preserve your psychological autonomy.

Foster more honest and respectful interactions.

Recognize and disarm manipulations without causing unnecessary harm.

Connection to Dark Psychology

Understanding how to protect yourself from manipulation is an indispensable complement to the ethical use of dark psychology. Just as influence can be used to shape behaviors, it must also be balanced with the ability to identify and neutralize unwanted influences.

Mastering this skill ensures that you remain in control of your choices and actions, safeguarding yourself against external interventions that could compromise your emotional and psychological integrity.

Chapter 44
Dark Psychology at Work

The workplace is a complex setting where dark psychology can be used to influence dynamics, build authority, negotiate effectively, and resolve conflicts. This chapter explores how to apply dark psychology techniques in a professional context strategically and ethically, examining methods to understand behaviors, shape perceptions, and achieve organizational or personal goals without compromising relationships or reputations.

Why is Dark Psychology Relevant at Work?

The workplace involves constant interactions among people with different goals, personalities, and priorities. Dark psychology allows you to:

Understand and Anticipate Behaviors

Identify action patterns and predict reactions during negotiations or conflicts.

Establish Authority and Respect

Project leadership and earn the trust of colleagues and subordinates.

Influence Decisions

Shape perceptions and drive favorable outcomes in projects and negotiations.

Resolve Conflicts

Redirect tensions and foster collaborative solutions.

Key Dark Psychology Techniques in the Workplace

Building Professional Rapport

Establish genuine connections through empathy and understanding others' needs.

Example: In a meeting, use open body language and a friendly tone to create a trusting environment.

Subtle Mirroring

Discreetly adopt the posture, speech rhythm, and gestures of colleagues or superiors to create subconscious empathy.

Using Positive Suggestions

Introduce ideas indirectly, shaping perceptions before decisions are made.

Example: "Many of us have noticed that this approach could save resources."

Establishing Authority Through Narratives

Craft stories that demonstrate competence and leadership, shaping how your team perceives you.

Example: "In a previous project, we faced a similar challenge and overcame it by applying this strategy."

Identifying Strategic Alliances

Spot key influencers within the team and build partnerships that strengthen your position.

Manipulating the Environment

Create a favorable setting for your objectives by adjusting physical or social elements.

Example: Arrange meetings in neutral environments to reduce perceived hierarchy or tension.

Creating Perceived Scarcity

Leverage limited time, resources, or opportunities to increase decision-making urgency.

Example: "We have until the end of the day to submit this proposal, or we might miss the opportunity."

Practical Applications in the Workplace

Negotiations and Meetings

Use persuasion techniques to align interests and reach favorable agreements.

Example: Begin by discussing points of agreement before introducing your main proposals.

Conflict Resolution

Identify underlying emotions and use empathy to diffuse tensions.

Example: "It seems like everyone is concerned about deadlines. Let's work together to find a practical solution."

Team Management

Apply leadership strategies to inspire and motivate the team.

Example: Reinforce positive behaviors by publicly recognizing specific members' efforts.

Promotion and Personal Growth

Highlight your achievements and demonstrate your value to the organization.

Example: When discussing a promotion, share tangible results you've achieved and link them to company goals.

Influence in Collaborative Projects

Steer the team's focus toward ideas or strategies that support your goals.

Example: Ask questions that guide the group to view your approach as the most logical.

Common Mistakes When Applying Dark Psychology at Work

Appearing Manipulative

Obvious tactics may lead to distrust or damage your reputation.

Solution: Maintain subtlety in all interactions.

Focusing Solely on Your Interests

Ignoring others' needs can result in resistance and isolation.

Solution: Balance your goals with clear benefits for others.

Overlooking Organizational Culture

Techniques effective in one environment may be misinterpreted in another.

Solution: Adapt your approaches to the organization's norms and values.

Overusing Authority

Over-assertiveness can be seen as arrogance or micromanagement.

Solution: Combine authority with humility and collaboration.

Recognizing Dark Psychology Used Against You at Work

Excessive Pressure for Quick Decisions

Assess if urgency is genuine or a manipulation tactic.

Subtle Criticism or Gaslighting

Watch for comments intended to undermine your confidence or competence.

Social Isolation

Note attempts to weaken your connections with colleagues.

Disinformation

Identify information manipulated to favor someone else.

Defense Strategies in the Workplace

Strengthen Key Relationships

Build alliances with trustworthy colleagues who can provide support or validation.

Maintain Transparent Communication

Document information and share important data with all involved.

Practice Assertiveness

Respond to manipulation calmly and firmly, reaffirming your viewpoints.

Demonstrate Competence and Reliability

Proactively showcase your value through consistent results.

Exercises to Practice Dark Psychology at Work

Observe Group Dynamics

Analyze team interactions and identify key influencers.

Practice Authority Narratives

Develop stories about your achievements that highlight leadership and competence.

Use Mirroring in Meetings

Experiment with subtle body language mirroring to build rapport with colleagues and superiors.

Plan Strategic Interventions

Create hypothetical scenarios and plan how to shape perceptions or resolve conflicts in those contexts.

The Ethics of Dark Psychology at Work

Using dark psychology in the workplace demands responsibility. Employ it to:

Resolve conflicts and promote collaboration.

Demonstrate leadership and inspire teams.

Influence decisions aligned with collective interests.

Avoid:

Manipulating colleagues for selfish gains.

Exploiting emotional vulnerabilities for unfair advantages.

Connecting with Dark Psychology

In the workplace, dark psychology provides a balance between building genuine connections and using strategic techniques to achieve goals. When applied with integrity, it transforms organizational challenges into opportunities for growth and positive impact. Mastering this skill allows you to navigate corporate dynamics confidently, shaping your career and strengthening your position in any professional context.

Chapter 45
Influence on Social Media

Social media is one of the most powerful arenas for applying dark psychology. It provides a space to disseminate ideas, shape perceptions, and build influence on a global scale. This chapter explores how principles of dark psychology can be applied to understand and manipulate behaviors on digital platforms. From creating content to recognizing influence strategies, this chapter offers a strategic approach to navigating this dynamic and potentially manipulative environment.

Why Are Social Media Platforms Fertile Ground for Dark Psychology?

Constant Immersion

Daily and continuous use of social media increases receptiveness to subtle messages.

Rapid Emotional Impact

Images, videos, and short texts are designed to provoke instant, often emotional reactions.

Perceived Personal Connection

Social media interactions create a false sense of closeness, facilitating influence.

Viral Dissemination

Ideas can spread quickly, reaching a vast audience with minimal effort.

Data and Algorithms

Platforms collect detailed user information, enabling personalized persuasive messages.

Influence Techniques on Social Media

Building Virtual Authority

Develop an online presence that conveys credibility and expertise in your field.

Example: Publish consistent, relevant, and well-researched content to establish yourself as a trusted voice.

Strategic Use of Emotions

Share stories or content that evoke strong emotions, such as empathy, anger, or enthusiasm.

Example: Motivational videos or social issues that deeply engage the audience.

Creating Scarcity and Exclusivity

Use phrases that generate a sense of urgency or limited access.

Example: "Offer valid only for the first 100 subscribers!"

Manipulating Social Proof

Show evidence of public approval, such as likes, shares, and positive comments, to reinforce your message.

Example: Highlight testimonials from satisfied users in posts about products or services.

Segmentation and Personalization

Tailor messages for different audiences based on their preferences and behaviors.

Using Mental Triggers

Include words or phrases that prompt specific actions from the audience.

Example: "Click now to change your life!"

Curating Narratives

Control the story being told about you or your content, emphasizing positive aspects and shaping perceptions.

Engaging Visual Stimuli

Use high-quality images and videos to capture attention and reinforce your message.

How to Strategically Apply Dark Psychology on Social Media

Define Your Goals

Determine what you aim to achieve, such as engagement, sales, or audience growth.

Understand Your Audience
Analyze your audience's interests, problems, and aspirations to adapt your content.

Plan Your Virtual Identity
Create a profile that conveys authenticity and authority, aligned with your target audience.

Strategically Engage Your Audience
Use questions, polls, or challenges to actively involve your audience.

Post Consistently
Maintain regularity to increase visibility and reinforce your message.

Leverage Algorithms
Study how platform algorithms work to maximize the reach of your posts.

Recognizing Influence Tactics on Social Media

Messages Evoking Fear or Urgency
Assess whether content appeals to insecurities or forces quick decisions.

Manipulation Through Reciprocity
Notice if you feel pressured to return a perceived favor, such as freebies or discounts.

Exaggerated Use of Emotions
Evaluate whether content intentionally amplifies situations to sway your opinion.

Overuse of Social Proof
Be cautious of accounts or campaigns with inflated numbers of likes or followers to create a false sense of popularity.

Protecting Yourself from Manipulation on Social Media

Practice Critical Thinking
Evaluate content skeptically and question the intentions behind posts or campaigns.

Verify Sources and Data
Ensure that shared information is based on credible sources.

Turn Off Unnecessary Notifications

Reduce exposure to constant stimuli that may direct your behavior.

Customize Your Settings

Adjust privacy preferences to limit data collection and exposure to targeted ads.

Avoid Impulsive Reactions

Reflect on the truth and impact of emotional content before reacting or sharing.

Risks of Using Dark Psychology on Social Media

Loss of Credibility

Manipulative tactics may be discovered, damaging your reputation.

Solution: Maintain authenticity and use influence ethically.

Over-Reliance on Algorithms

Depending solely on algorithms can limit creativity and organic reach.

Solution: Diversify strategies to engage your audience directly.

Content Saturation

Excessive posting may fatigue your audience and reduce impact.

Solution: Prioritize quality over quantity.

Exercises to Apply Influence Strategies on Social Media

Create a Content Calendar

Plan posts based on specific goals, such as engagement or sales.

Analyze Successful Campaigns

Study viral posts and identify the elements that made them impactful.

Test Different Formats

Experiment with videos, carousels, polls, and live streams to determine what works best for your audience.

Monitor Relevant Metrics

Track likes, comments, shares, and conversion rates to adjust your strategies.

Ethics in Using Dark Psychology on Social Media

Using dark psychology on social media requires responsibility. Employ it to:

Educate and inspire your audience authentically.

Promote messages that benefit your followers and community.

Build relationships based on trust and respect.

Avoid:

Manipulating emotions dishonestly for selfish gains.

Spreading false or misleading information.

Connecting with Dark PsychologySocial media reflects human psychology in action, amplifying opportunities for influence and manipulation. Mastering the tactics described in this chapter enables you to actively participate in this environment, whether to strengthen your digital presence, protect yourself from manipulation, or achieve strategic goals.

By applying these techniques intelligently and with integrity, you can maximize your impact without compromising the ethical principles that underpin healthy and productive interactions.

Chapter 46
Creating Magnetic Charisma

Magnetic charisma is the ability to attract and influence people effortlessly, evoking admiration, trust, and connection. This chapter explores the psychological components of charisma and how to cultivate it intentionally. In the context of dark psychology, creating magnetic charisma goes beyond mere likability; it involves developing a presence that inspires and motivates while maintaining control over social interactions.

What Is Magnetic Charisma?

Magnetic charisma is not an innate quality but a combination of traits that can be learned and enhanced. It involves:

Authenticity

The ability to be genuine and sincere, fostering a true connection with others.

Unshakable Confidence

A confident presence that conveys security and leadership.

Communication Skills

Effective use of words, body language, and expressions to engage and influence.

Active Empathy

Showing genuine interest in the needs and feelings of others.

Positive Energy

The ability to inspire enthusiasm and optimism in those around you.

Why Is Charisma Powerful?

Magnetic charisma is a powerful psychological tool because it directly influences people's subconscious:

Increases Social Attractiveness
Charismatic individuals are perceived as trustworthy, competent, and inspiring.

Creates Rapid Connections
Facilitates the building of solid relationships in less time.

Establishes Natural Authority
Charismatic people are seen as natural leaders, even in informal settings.

Shapes Perceptions and Behaviors
Makes it easier to subtly influence decisions and actions.

Components of Magnetic Charisma

Presence
Be fully present in every interaction, giving your complete attention to the moment and the person.

Powerful Communication
Use stories, metaphors, and a controlled tone of voice to captivate attention.

Self-Confidence
Display self-belief through upright posture, firm gestures, and consistent eye contact.

Strategic Humility
Show vulnerability and humility to reinforce authenticity and empathy.

Contagious Enthusiasm
Inspire enthusiasm with positive energy and a genuine smile.

Techniques to Cultivate Magnetic Charisma

Practice Active Listening
Give full attention to what others say, validating their feelings and ideas.
Example: Repeat or rephrase what the person shared to show you truly understand.

Master Body Language
Use open gestures, consistent eye contact, and facial expressions that reinforce your words.

Tell Engaging Stories
Share narratives that evoke emotion and create connection.
Example: Relate a personal moment that resonates with your audience's values.
Project Confidence in Your Voice
Speak clearly, maintaining a calm and assertive pace.
Show Genuine Interest
Ask open-ended questions and show curiosity about others' experiences and opinions.
Incorporate Humor
Use appropriate humor to ease tensions and foster a friendly atmosphere.
Express Gratitude and Recognition
Publicly acknowledge others' contributions, building deeper bonds.
Practical Examples of Magnetic Charisma
In Job Interviews
Combine confidence with curiosity by asking intelligent questions and showing genuine enthusiasm for the opportunity.
In Business Meetings
Use stories and metaphors to present ideas, keeping the audience engaged and inspired.
On Social Media
Project authenticity through personal interactions and responses that value your followers.
In Personal Relationships
Demonstrate mindfulness and empathy to build deep and lasting connections.
Common Mistakes When Trying to Be Charismatic
Overexertion
Forcing charisma can feel artificial and repel people.
Solution: Focus on being genuine and authentic.
Lack of Consistency
Inconsistent behaviors can undermine trust.
Solution: Ensure your actions align with your words.
Ignoring the Audience

Focusing solely on yourself can alienate others.

Solution: Pay equal attention to the needs and perspectives of others.

Excessive Confidence

Overconfidence can be perceived as arrogance.

Solution: Balance confidence with humility.

Exercises to Develop Magnetic Charisma

Train Body Language

Practice open gestures and confident postures in front of a mirror.

Record Your Interactions

Review recordings of conversations or presentations to identify areas for improvement.

Develop Personal Stories

Craft narratives that demonstrate overcoming challenges, learning, or showing empathy.

Practice Positive Feedback

Get into the habit of sincerely and specifically praising others.

How to Recognize and Respond to Manipulative Charismatic People

Analyze Intentions

Ask yourself whether the charisma is being used for mutual benefit or selfish gain.

Stay Alert

Do not confuse charisma with competence or integrity; seek concrete evidence of the person's intentions.

Set Boundaries

Do not let someone's charm compromise your values or goals.

Ethics in Using Magnetic Charisma

Charisma is a powerful tool that should be used responsibly. Use it to:

Inspire and motivate others.

Resolve conflicts constructively.

Build relationships based on trust and mutual respect.

Avoid:

Exploiting vulnerabilities or abusing people's trust.

Using charisma to deceive or coerce.

The Connection to Dark Psychology

Creating magnetic charisma is a skill that integrates various dark psychology techniques, from strategic empathy to controlled emotional expression. When aligned with ethical purposes, charisma transforms social interactions into opportunities to lead, influence, and deeply connect with others.

Mastering this skill allows you to exert influence in a powerful and positive way, becoming a figure who attracts and inspires with effortless grace.

Chapter 47
Seduction Techniques

Seduction is a form of influence deeply rooted in human psychology. Beyond romantic or sexual attraction, seduction is the ability to captivate and win another person's attention, interest, and trust. This chapter explores how seduction techniques can be strategically applied in various social contexts, using psychological principles to create connections, evoke emotions, and shape perceptions.

What Is Seduction?

Seduction is the process of attracting someone through a combination of charisma, communication, and understanding their emotional needs. In the context of dark psychology, it is used to create a profound impact in social interactions, always considering the ethics of its application.

The Psychological Foundations of Seduction

Emotional Appeal

Seduction operates in the realm of emotions, evoking feelings of curiosity, desire, or admiration.

Reciprocity

When someone perceives that you offer something valuable—attention, praise, or affection—they naturally feel inclined to reciprocate.

Mystery

The unknown or partially revealed sparks curiosity, creating a desire to know more.

Proximity and Familiarity

Positive and frequent contact increases the likelihood of forming a seductive connection.

Subjective Validation

Showing that you understand and appreciate the other person's emotions or values strengthens the bond.

Essential Traits of a Seductive Person

Confidence

Self-confidence is irresistible; it communicates competence and emotional stability.

Authenticity

Being genuine fosters a sense of safety and trustworthiness in interactions.

Charm and Humor

Charm combines likability and grace, while humor eases tensions and creates an enjoyable atmosphere.

Empathy

The ability to put yourself in another's shoes allows you to connect with their needs and desires.

Engaging Communication

A seductive person knows how to use words, gestures, and expressions to captivate and engage.

Applied Seduction Techniques

Subtle Mirroring

Reflect the other person's behavior, tone of voice, or posture to create a subconscious sense of connection.

Creating Intrigue

Reveal information gradually, maintaining an air of mystery that piques curiosity.

Example: Share an intriguing experience but leave the ending open, inviting questions.

Emotional Validation

Show that you understand and respect the other person's emotions, reinforcing the emotional bond.

Personalized Compliments

Go beyond generic praise and highlight specific qualities you admire.

Example: "I admire how you can explain complex ideas so clearly."

Subtly Calculated Touches

When appropriate and respectful, touch can strengthen emotional connection.

Example: A firm handshake, a touch on the shoulder, or a brief gesture of approval.

Strategic Eye Contact

Maintain eye contact at key moments to convey sincerity and interest.

Creating Exclusivity

Make the person feel special or unique in your life.

Example: "I've never met someone who thinks about this topic the way you do."

Applications of Seduction in Various Contexts

In Professional Settings

Use seduction techniques to build relationships, strengthen connections, and inspire trust.

Example: In a negotiation, demonstrate genuine interest in the other party's needs, fostering collaboration.

In Personal Relationships

Deepen emotional bonds by showing understanding, support, and authentic interest.

In Social Media Building

Captivate audiences through engaging storytelling, authenticity, and a magnetic presence.

In Leadership Roles

Inspire and motivate your team with an empathetic, charismatic, and visionary approach.

Common Mistakes in Seduction

Overexertion

Forcing seduction can come across as desperation or manipulation.

Solution: Stay natural and let the interaction flow.

Ignoring Boundaries

Pushing too far without respecting the other person's space or preferences can drive them away.

Solution: Observe their reactions and adjust your approach.

Lack of Authenticity

Artificial or exaggerated behavior undermines trust.

Solution: Be sincere and consistent with your values and intentions.

Excessive Mystery

Being overly reserved can frustrate and discourage the other person's interest.

Solution: Reveal information at a balanced pace.

How to Resist Manipulative Seduction

Analyze Intentions

Ask yourself whether the attention you're receiving is genuine or strategic.

Observe Patterns

Notice if the person uses the same seduction techniques with others, indicating a lack of authenticity.

Trust Your Intuition

If something feels forced or manipulative, trust your instincts.

Set Boundaries

Be clear about what is acceptable and unacceptable in the interaction.

Exercises to Practice Seduction Techniques

Practice Eye Contact

Train yourself to maintain comfortable eye contact without being intimidating.

Develop Engaging Stories

Create personal narratives that showcase your unique qualities and memorable experiences.

Improve Your Body Language

Practice open postures, natural gestures, and friendly facial expressions.

Listen Actively

Dedicate yourself to listening without interruptions, showing genuine interest.

Ethics in Seduction

Seduction should be used respectfully and ethically, prioritizing the well-being and autonomy of those involved. Use it to:

Build genuine connections.
Inspire trust and admiration.
Strengthen relationships authentically.

Avoid:

Using seduction to manipulate or exploit vulnerabilities.
Forcing connections or disregarding boundaries.

The Connection to Dark Psychology

Seduction integrates key elements of dark psychology, such as empathy, persuasion, and emotional control. When used responsibly, it becomes a powerful tool for creating meaningful bonds and exerting influence subtly and effectively.

Mastering seduction techniques enables you to captivate and connect with people on a deeper level, fostering interactions that benefit everyone involved.

Chapter 48
Impression Management

Managing the impression others have of you is a strategic skill that influences how you are perceived and treated in various social, professional, and personal contexts. In the realm of dark psychology, impression management involves consciously controlling the signals you emit to subtly but powerfully shape others' perceptions. This chapter delves into the techniques, psychological foundations, and practical applications of this skill.

What is Impression Management?

Impression management is the process of adjusting your behavior, appearance, and communication to create a desired perception in others. This includes controlling elements such as:

Body Language

Gestures, posture, and expressions that reinforce your message.

Verbal Communication

Choice of words, tone of voice, and conversational style.

Physical Appearance

Clothing, hygiene, and style that influence how you are judged.

Behavioral Interactions

Attitudes and actions that demonstrate specific values and intentions.

Why is Impression Management Important?

Control of Social Perception

Shaping how you are perceived can facilitate relationships, partnerships, and opportunities.

Increased Influence

A good impression builds trust and authority, making it easier to persuade and inspire others.

Reputation Building

Creates a consistent and respectable image across different environments.

Conflict Reduction

Well-managed presentations minimize misunderstandings and interpersonal conflicts.

The Psychological Foundations of Impression Management

Primacy Effect

First impressions have a lasting impact and shape how future behaviors are interpreted.

Cognitive Consistency

People prefer consistent perceptions; strong initial signals are reinforced over time.

Confirmation Bias

A good initial impression leads others to seek information that confirms that perception.

Projection of Status and Power

Visual and behavioral elements signal hierarchy and competence subconsciously.

Techniques for Impression Management

Body Language Control

Posture: Stand upright to project confidence and presence.

Gestures: Use smooth and controlled movements to convey calm and security.

Eye Contact: Establish and maintain appropriate eye contact to demonstrate sincerity.

Appropriate Appearance for Context

Dress according to the environment and the message you wish to convey.

Example: Formal attire to inspire authority; stylish casual wear for approachability.

Choice of Words
Use clear, articulate communication tailored to the audience's level.

Use of Titles and Credentials
Highlight relevant qualifications to reinforce authority and trustworthiness.

Alignment of Verbal and Non-Verbal Cues
Ensure that your body language matches your spoken message.

Social Media Management
Present yourself consistently and strategically on digital platforms, focusing on credibility and authenticity.

Eliciting Positive Feedback
Seek constructive opinions and show interest in improvement, strengthening your image as approachable and open.

Examples of Impression Management in Different Contexts

Job Interviews
Dress professionally and demonstrate moderated enthusiasm.

Speak about your achievements objectively and clearly.

Social Settings
Be approachable and friendly while maintaining a confident and authentic posture.

Use light humor to create connections.

Professional Leadership
Show confidence and empathy when making decisions or giving feedback.

Use narratives that reinforce your vision and values.

Public Speaking
Use confident posture and vocal modulation to hold the audience's attention.

Prepare thoroughly to convey credibility and mastery of the subject.

Common Mistakes in Impression Management

Inconsistency
Contradictory behaviors undermine credibility.
Solution: Ensure your actions align with your message.
Excessive Focus on Appearance
Relying solely on appearance may seem superficial.
Solution: Combine good presentation with solid skills and attitudes.
Trying Too Hard to Impress
Over-efforting to please can appear artificial.
Solution: Be authentic and avoid exaggerations.
Neglecting Digital Presence
An incoherent online presence can harm your overall image.
Solution: Regularly monitor your social media and adjust content as needed.

How to Resist Impression Management Techniques Directed at You
Focus on Facts
Evaluate concrete outcomes rather than relying solely on initial presentations.
Look for Inconsistencies
Observe discrepancies between words and actions that may indicate manipulation.
Question Credentials
Verify the validity of highlighted titles or achievements.
Trust Your Intuition
If something feels forced or artificial, investigate further.

Exercises to Practice Impression Management
Appearance Testing
Experiment with different styles of clothing in various situations and observe reactions.
Body Language Practice
Train posture, gestures, and expressions in front of a mirror or record interactions for later analysis.
Social Simulations

Attend events or meetings and apply specific techniques such as eye contact and active listening.

Crafting Personal Stories

Develop narratives that highlight your achievements and values in an engaging way.

Ethics in Impression Management

While impression management is a powerful tool, it should be used with integrity. Use it to:

Project an image consistent with your skills and values.

Facilitate genuine connections and collaborations.

Inspire trust and respect in social and professional interactions.

Avoid:

Creating a false or misleading persona to manipulate others.

Using techniques to mask dishonest intentions or harm others.

Connection to Dark Psychology

Impression management is one of the most practical and versatile applications of dark psychology. It allows you to control the narrative of how you are perceived, using subtlety and strategy to shape behaviors and achieve specific goals.

Mastering this skill ensures you have control over your image, opening doors to relationships, opportunities, and influence that align with your purposes and values.

Chapter 49
Psychology in Financial Decisions

Psychology plays a crucial role in financial decisions, shaping how people perceive risks, value rewards, and prioritize choices. This chapter explores how principles of dark psychology can be applied to influence transactions, negotiations, and financial behaviors in personal or professional contexts. It also addresses how to identify and resist financial manipulations, protecting yourself from impulsive or unfavorable decisions.

The Role of Psychology in Finance

Financial decisions are rarely purely rational. They are heavily influenced by:

Emotions

Feelings like fear, greed, or excitement affect the willingness to take risks.

Cognitive Biases

Distorted perceptions, such as overvaluing immediate gains over future benefits, alter choices.

Social Influence

Group pressure can lead to conformity, even in personal financial decisions.

Lack of Information

Ambiguity or insufficient knowledge increases vulnerability to manipulation.

Principles of Dark Psychology in Financial Decisions

Anchoring

The first piece of information presented in a negotiation or transaction strongly influences the perceived value.

Example: Offering a high initial price makes discounts seem more attractive.

Scarcity Effect

Creating a sense of urgency or rarity increases the desire for a product or service.

Example: "Offer valid only today!"

Social Proof

Showing that others are buying or investing reinforces the decision as safe or advantageous.

Example: "Thousands of customers have already chosen this plan."

Conditional Rewards

Offering incentives for quick decisions, like bonuses or gifts, pressures action.

Example: "Sign up now and get one month free."

Appeal to Authority

Using experts or prominent figures to validate a financial choice.

Example: "Recommended by the market's top analysts."

Commitment Effect

Getting someone to accept a small concession initially increases the likelihood of larger commitments later.

Example: "Invest just $10 today and see how it works before increasing your contribution."

Applying Dark Psychology Techniques in Financial Contexts

Negotiations

Use anchoring to establish a favorable initial position, shaping the other side's expectations.

Sales and Marketing

Include elements of scarcity, social proof, and rewards to encourage purchases or subscriptions.

Creating Attractive Proposals

Present options in a way that makes the desired choice appear the most logical or advantageous.

Example: Offer three plans, with the middle option labeled as the "best choice."

Using Narratives

Share stories about people who succeeded by making similar decisions, creating an emotional connection.

Managing Financial Conflicts

Redirect financial objections toward intangible values such as security, trust, or exclusivity.

Common Mistakes in Influencing Financial Decisions

Excessive Pressure

Over-insistence can create resistance or mistrust.

Solution: Balance persuasion with room for reflection.

Unrealistic Promises

Overstated guarantees can damage credibility.

Solution: Be transparent and honest about risks and benefits.

Ignoring Individual Contexts

Overlooking the other party's specific needs or circumstances can drive them away.

Solution: Tailor approaches to the other party's priorities.

Overreliance on Psychological Triggers

Obvious manipulations may be perceived as dishonest.

Solution: Use triggers subtly and respectfully.

Recognizing Manipulations in Financial Decisions Against You

Manufactured Urgency

Question tight deadlines meant to force quick decisions.

Exclusive Focus on Benefits

Be wary of promises that ignore risks or challenges.

Overblown Social Proof

Verify the authenticity of testimonials or statistics presented.

Conditional Rewards Tied to Commitment

Carefully evaluate whether the incentives justify the decision.

Omitted Information
Ask for clarification on financial aspects that were not addressed.

Strategies to Resist Financial Manipulations
Ask for Time to Reflect
Avoid financial decisions under pressure.
Research Alternatives
Compare offers and explore options before committing.
Trust Concrete Data
Base your decisions on clear numbers and analysis, rather than emotional appeals.
Set Boundaries
Establish a budget or clear criteria for investments and purchases.
Consult Experts
Seek impartial advice from trusted professionals.

Exercises to Practice Psychology in Financial Decisions
Negotiation Simulations
Practice setting anchors and addressing objections in fictional scenarios.
Creating Persuasive Proposals
Develop sales or marketing strategies that incorporate psychological triggers.
Analyzing Real-Life Cases
Study successful financial campaigns to identify the techniques used.
Self-Assessment of Financial Decisions
Reflect on your past choices to recognize psychological influences.

Ethics in Financial Psychology
When applying dark psychology in financial decisions, ethical considerations are crucial. Use these techniques to:
Help others make informed decisions aligned with their goals.

Offer legitimate and transparent solutions.

Build financial relationships based on trust and mutual respect.

Avoid:

Exploiting others' ignorance or financial vulnerability.

Omitting critical information or distorting reality.

Connection to Dark Psychology

The application of psychology in financial decisions exemplifies how subtle influences strategically shape behaviors. Mastering these techniques allows you to navigate negotiations and transactions with confidence, shaping outcomes that meet your goals while promoting mutual benefits.

When used ethically, this skill not only enhances your effectiveness in financial contexts but also strengthens your credibility and positive impact in economic interactions.

Chapter 50
Mass Influence

Influencing large groups is a powerful and complex skill that requires a deep understanding of collective psychology. Unlike individual manipulation, mass influence focuses on creating messages or actions that resonate broadly, leveraging social behaviors and group dynamics. This chapter explores dark psychology techniques applied to mass influence, addressing strategic methods for mobilizing audiences, shaping opinions, and achieving large-scale goals.

What Is Mass Influence?

Mass influence is the ability to shape behaviors, beliefs, or decisions of large groups of people, whether at a live event, on social media, or through marketing campaigns. This skill is based on:

Group Dynamics

Individuals often behave differently within a group than they would individually.

Social Norms

Social expectations within a group shape collective behavior.

Collective Emotions

Shared emotions, such as enthusiasm or outrage, amplify receptiveness to a message.

Charismatic Leadership

The perceived authority or charisma of a leader strengthens acceptance of their ideas.

Why Is Mass Influence Powerful?

Broader Reach

Affecting many people simultaneously can lead to significant social or institutional changes.

Multiplier Effect

A compelling message can spread through shares, discussions, and spontaneous reactions.

Unity and Action

Influenced groups can be mobilized toward specific goals, such as supporting causes or adopting desired behaviors.

Perception Shift

Large-scale messaging can reshape narratives or preexisting beliefs.

Techniques for Mass Influence

Use Simple and Powerful Messages

Short, impactful phrases are easier to remember and share.

Example: "Just do it." (Nike).

Create Collective Emotions

Present stories or images that evoke empathy, outrage, or pride.

Example: Humanitarian campaigns showcasing people in need.

Leverage Influencers

Use respected or charismatic figures to validate and amplify your message.

Reinforce Group Identity

Build a sense of belonging around your message.

Example: "Join the movement!"

Appeal to Scarcity

Convey a sense of urgency to prompt immediate action.

Example: "Last days to register!"

Strategic Repetition

Repeat your message consistently to enhance memorability and acceptance.

Utilize Social Proof

Show how others have already joined or supported your cause.

Example: "Over 1 million people already participate."

Leverage Live Events

Mobilize people through speeches, protests, or live broadcasts, creating shared experiences.

Collective Psychology in Mass Influence

Herd Behavior

People tend to follow majority decisions in uncertain situations.

Social Conformity

The need to align with group expectations facilitates message acceptance.

Group Polarization

Groups often adopt more extreme positions after collective discussions.

Emotional Contagion

Emotions, especially negative ones, spread rapidly within groups.

Practical Examples of Mass Influence

Advertising Campaigns

Messages using repetition, scarcity, and emotion are more effective at attracting consumers.

Social Movements

Charismatic leaders and powerful slogans mobilize people around specific causes.

Political Campaigns

Speeches appealing to national identity or hope shape large-scale opinions.

Digital Marketing

Social platforms allow for audience segmentation to deliver more personalized and impactful messages.

Common Mistakes in Attempting Mass Influence

Complex or Ambiguous Messages

These can confuse and weaken the impact.

Solution: Simplify your message for clarity and immediate understanding.

Lack of Emotional Connection

Purely rational messages tend to be less memorable.

Solution: Combine facts with emotional narratives.

Misalignment with Audience Values

Ideas that contradict core beliefs face higher resistance.

Solution: Thoroughly research the audience's motivations before crafting the message.

Exaggeration or Falsehoods

Overpromising or misleading information can ruin credibility.

Solution: Be honest and transparent in presenting arguments.

How to Identify and Resist Mass Influence

Question Intentions

Assess who is promoting the message and their potential interests.

Analyze Evidence

Seek concrete data supporting the claims made.

Recognize Emotional Triggers

Determine whether the message manipulates emotions to influence choices.

Consult Diverse Sources

Compare various perspectives to avoid being swayed by a single narrative.

Exercises to Practice Mass Influence

Create Campaigns

Develop a fictional campaign to test your ability to engage large groups.

Case Studies

Analyze historical examples of mass influence, such as political or social campaigns, to identify techniques used.

Team Simulations

Practice influencing small groups with structured and emotional messages.

Audience Feedback

Present ideas to different audiences and evaluate their reactions to refine your approach.

Ethics in Mass Influence

Influencing large groups demands responsibility. Use this skill to:

Promote positive and constructive changes.

Mobilize people for legitimate and ethical causes.

Facilitate understanding and collaboration on important issues.

Avoid:

Manipulating emotions for selfish or harmful gains.

Dividing or polarizing groups intentionally to create chaos.

The Connection to Dark Psychology

Mass influence is the culmination of various dark psychology techniques applied strategically and at scale. When used ethically, it provides a powerful tool to shape perceptions, mobilize audiences, and positively impact society.

Mastering this skill enables you to lead and influence on a global scale, guiding groups toward meaningful and transformative goals.

Chapter 51
Developing Mental Resilience

Mental resilience is the ability to withstand, recover from, and thrive in the face of adversity and external manipulations. In the context of dark psychology, it is essential for fortifying the mind against attempts at control and influence. This chapter explores how to cultivate a resilient mindset through psychological techniques, daily practices, and self-awareness strategies, creating a strong defense against manipulation and pressure.

What is Mental Resilience?

Mental resilience is the ability to maintain emotional stability, clarity of thought, and decision-making control in challenging or manipulative situations.

Emotional Control

The ability to manage intense emotions and avoid impulsive reactions.

Self-Awareness

Recognizing and understanding your own thoughts and feelings to make more informed decisions.

Adaptability

Flexibility to adjust to new circumstances without compromising values or goals.

Persistence

Continuing to move forward despite obstacles or temporary setbacks.

Why is Mental Resilience Essential?

Protection Against Manipulation

Reduces vulnerability to emotional or social control tactics.

Strengthening Autonomy

Helps you align your choices with your own interests and values.

Improved Well-Being

Minimizes the impact of stress and external pressure on mental and emotional health.

Increased Confidence

Empowers you to face challenges assertively and securely.

Techniques to Develop Mental Resilience

Recognize Your Vulnerabilities

Identify areas where you feel most susceptible to manipulation or stress.

Example: Do you easily react to praise or criticism?

Practice Emotional Control

Develop techniques to manage emotional reactions, such as deep breathing or mindfulness.

Example: When feeling angry or anxious, stop and breathe deeply for a few minutes.

Build a Support Network

Connect with people who offer honest and constructive support, strengthening your confidence and perspective.

Develop Critical Thinking

Question information and intuitions before making important decisions.

Example: Ask yourself, "What evidence supports this claim?"

Strengthen Your Boundaries

Learn to say "no" assertively and establish clear boundaries in personal and professional relationships.

Cultivate Mindfulness

Practice being present in the moment and observing your thoughts without judgment. This helps reduce automatic reactions.

Learn from Experience

Reflect on past situations to identify behavioral patterns that can be adjusted.

How to Protect Yourself from Manipulation with Mental Resilience

Recognize Emotional Triggers

Identify situations that provoke strong reactions and associated vulnerabilities.

Example: A sense of urgency in a sales pitch might trigger impulsivity.

Create Space for Decisions

Whenever possible, delay responses or actions to gain mental clarity.

Practice Self-Control

Build the ability to pause before reacting, especially in emotionally charged situations.

Educate Yourself About Manipulation Techniques

The more you know, the easier it is to recognize and neutralize control attempts.

Monitor Your Inner Dialogue

Observe automatic negative thoughts and replace them with constructive narratives.

Practical Exercises to Build Mental Resilience

Emotion Journal

Keep a diary to note challenging situations, how you felt, and how you reacted.

Gratitude Practice

List three things you are grateful for daily to cultivate a positive mindset.

Breathing Techniques

Practice breathing exercises to remain calm during stressful moments.

Scenario Simulation

Imagine high-pressure scenarios and rehearse assertive responses.

Common Mistakes in Developing Mental Resilience

Ignoring Emotions

Suppressing feelings can lead to stronger reactions later.

Solution: Acknowledge and process your emotions instead of ignoring them.

Focusing Only on the Negative

Dwelling on failures or challenges can undermine your confidence.

Solution: Balance your analysis with recognition of your strengths.

Pursuing Perfection

Resilience doesn't mean being infallible but learning from mistakes and continuing to grow.

Solution: Embrace imperfections as part of growth.

Isolation

Trying to handle everything alone can increase stress and limit perspectives.

Solution: Seek support and feedback from trusted people.

The Ethics of Mental Resilience

Mental resilience should be used to:

Protect your emotional and psychological autonomy.

Handle adversity constructively.

Inspire others to develop their inner strength.

Avoid:

Using your resilience to ignore the needs or feelings of others.

Becoming overly rigid or inflexible in your approach.

The Connection to Dark Psychology

Mental resilience is the armor against the influences of dark psychology. It allows you to identify manipulation, resist external pressures, and maintain emotional balance even in challenging scenarios.

By mastering this skill, you not only protect yourself but also create a solid foundation for influencing others with confidence and ethics. Mental resilience is the cornerstone of a strengthened mind, capable of thriving in any environment, no matter how adverse.

Chapter 52
Long-Term Strategies

While many dark psychology tactics are applied to achieve immediate results, long-term strategies offer a more sustainable and impactful approach to shaping behaviors, building relationships, and achieving complex goals. This chapter explores how to plan and implement dark psychology techniques with a long-term vision, emphasizing the importance of patience, consistency, and adaptability to context.

Why Are Long-Term Strategies Important?

Building Lasting Trust

Relationships and influences developed over time are stronger and more reliable.

Subtle and Effective Manipulation

A gradual approach allows influences to appear natural, reducing resistance.

Greater Control Over Outcomes

With enough time, you can adjust and refine your tactics as needed.

Sustainable Impact

Lasting changes are more effective for consolidating personal or professional goals.

Fundamental Principles of Long-Term Strategies

Detailed Planning

Structure your actions in clear steps, with well-defined intermediate and final goals.

Patience and Persistence

Accept that results may take time and avoid pressure for quick solutions.

Constant Adaptation
Reevaluate the context and adjust tactics as circumstances or the target's behavior changes.

Relationship Building
Invest in genuine connections that create fertile ground for future influence.

Consistency
Maintain actions aligned with your goals, reinforcing desired perceptions.

Components of a Successful Long-Term Strategy

Identification of Core Goals
Clearly define what you want to achieve and what results you consider acceptable.
Example: Shaping a group's opinion on a cause or building authority in a specific field.

Audience Segmentation
Understand who the key people or groups are that directly influence your objectives.

Creation of Coherent Narratives
Develop stories and messages that reinforce your values and goals over time.

Building Credibility
Demonstrate knowledge, reliability, and consistency to gradually earn trust.

Use of Progress Milestones
Establish checkpoints along the way to measure the effectiveness of your actions.

Dark Psychology Techniques Applied to the Long Term

Gradual Conditioning
Introduce changes or influences incrementally to avoid resistance.
Example: Gradually adjusting expectations or behaviors in a workplace setting.

Consistent Positive Reinforcement
Reward behaviors or decisions aligned with your goals to encourage future alignment.

Creating Emotional or Intellectual Dependence
Position yourself as an indispensable source of support, guidance, or validation.

Example: A mentor subtly guiding a mentee's strategic decisions.

Controlling Narratives Over Time
Position yourself as a central figure in stories that shape collective perceptions.

Using Psychosocial Triggers
Activate specific emotions or reactions to reinforce connections and maintain influence.

Practical Examples of Long-Term Strategies

Business Leadership

Establish an inspiring vision for your team and reinforce it consistently through actions and words.

Develop internal talent to ensure loyalty and continuity.

Brand Marketing
Create campaigns that reinforce values and messages over years, building consumer loyalty.

Building Personal Relationships
Invest time in authentic connections, creating trust and emotional dependence over time.

Political or Social Influence
Develop educational or engagement campaigns to gradually shift public opinions.

Common Mistakes in Long-Term Strategies

Lack of Clear Planning
The absence of specific goals can lead to disconnected and ineffective actions.

Solution: Structure your goals and tactics in detail.

Inconsistency
Contradictory behaviors can harm your credibility and efforts.

Solution: Keep your actions aligned over time.

Excessive Haste

Forcing results can generate resistance and compromise the strategy.
Solution: Respect the natural pace of change and progress.
Neglecting Feedback
Ignoring signals or reactions can lead to poorly adjusted strategies.
Solution: Continuously monitor and evaluate your actions.

How to Measure the Success of Your Long-Term Strategies
Evaluate Intermediate Results
Compare your progress milestones with the initial goals set.
Observe Behavioral Changes
Analyze whether the target individuals or groups are behaving as expected.
Monitor Reactions and Feelings
Assess how your influence is perceived and adjusted over time.
Identify Persistent Obstacles
Determine recurring patterns of resistance and develop tactics to overcome them.
Exercises to Practice Long-Term Strategies
Scenario Planning
Develop different scenarios to achieve a goal and identify the best tactics for each.
Progress Journal
Record your actions, observations, and results over time to identify patterns of success or failure.
Strategy Simulations
Practice implementing long-term strategies in fictional or controlled interactions.
Case Studies
Analyze historical or current examples of people or organizations that successfully implemented long-term strategies.
Ethics in Long-Term Strategies

Long-term strategies should be employed with integrity, using patience and planning to create a positive and lasting impact. Use them to:

Build strong, mutually beneficial relationships.

Promote constructive changes aligned with ethical values.

Inspire genuine trust and collaboration.

Avoid:

Using these strategies to exploit or harm others' vulnerabilities.

Prioritizing your goals at the expense of others' autonomy or well-being.

The Connection to Dark Psychology

Long-term strategies represent the most sophisticated application of dark psychology. They require a balance between patience and precise execution, combining subtle tactics to achieve lasting results. Mastering these strategies allows you to transform your approach to influence, shaping relationships and narratives over time in an ethical, strategic, and profoundly effective way.

Chapter 53
Ethics in Dark Psychology

The application of dark psychology concepts carries profound ethical implications. While the techniques presented throughout this book can be powerful tools for influencing behaviors and shaping decisions, the impact of your actions demands responsibility and awareness. This chapter explores the ethical dilemmas related to dark psychology, helping you establish clear boundaries between legitimate and abusive use of these strategies.

Why Is Ethics Essential in Dark Psychology?

Moral Responsibility

The power to influence behaviors should not be exercised selfishly or harmfully.

Building Strong Relationships

Unethical manipulation can breed distrust and destroy relationships in the long term.

Reputation and Credibility

Manipulative and dishonest actions compromise your personal and professional image.

Positive Social Impact

The ethical application of influence techniques can contribute to beneficial outcomes in communities and organizations.

The Foundations of Ethics in Dark Psychology

Autonomy

Respect the right of individuals to make informed decisions free from coercion or manipulation.

Beneficence

Use techniques to promote real benefits while avoiding harm.

Justice

Ensure your actions do not favor one group or individual at the expense of others.

Transparency

Maintain honesty about your intentions and methods whenever possible.

The Difference Between Ethical and Unethical Manipulation

Ethical Manipulation

Respects the individual's autonomy.

Aims to benefit all parties involved.

Is based on trust and mutual respect.

Unethical Manipulation

Exploits vulnerabilities or emotions selfishly.

Seeks personal gain regardless of its impact on others.

Violates or disregards implicit agreements of respect and integrity.

Examples of Ethical and Unethical Scenarios

Ethical Scenario

A manager uses persuasion techniques to motivate their team to meet goals, ensuring that the benefits are shared equally.

Unethical Scenario

A salesperson manipulates the emotions of a vulnerable customer to convince them to buy an expensive, unnecessary product.

Ethical Scenario

A friend uses mirroring techniques to provide emotional support, helping someone overcome a difficult moment.

Unethical Scenario

Someone pretends to be sympathetic and understanding to extract personal information and use it against the other person.

Common Dilemmas in the Application of Dark Psychology

Using Tactics in High-Pressure Situations

Ethical Question: Is it appropriate to use manipulation to achieve a critical goal, even if it harms third parties?

Ethical Response: Assess whether the benefit justifies the potential harm and seek less invasive alternatives.

Controlling Narratives

Ethical Question: Is shaping perceptions to protect your reputation or interests fair?

Ethical Response: Avoid distorting facts or deliberately misleading others.

Using Social Proof

Ethical Question: Is it acceptable to exaggerate the support you receive to influence decisions?

Ethical Response: Do not create artificial social proof; it undermines trust.

Techniques for Staying Within Ethical Boundaries

Define Your Intentions

Before applying any technique, ask yourself:

Am I seeking mutual benefit?

Does my action respect the other person's autonomy?

Reflect on the Consequences

Analyze how your actions might impact those involved in the short and long term.

Seek Feedback

Consult trusted individuals to evaluate whether your approach is ethical.

Set Personal Limits

Determine how far you are willing to go to achieve your goals while maintaining integrity.

Embrace Transparency Whenever Possible

Honesty strengthens trust and reduces misunderstandings.

How to Recognize Unethical Manipulation in Others

Excessive Pressure

Attempts to force an immediate decision often indicate manipulation.

Withholding Information

Deliberate omission of important facts is a sign of unethical behavior.

Appeals to Fear or Guilt

Tactics that exploit insecurities to gain compliance are manipulative.

Unrealistic Promises

Exaggerated guarantees or distortions of reality indicate ill intent.

Exercises to Practice Ethics in Dark Psychology

Case Analysis

Study examples of ethical and unethical influences and discuss how you would approach each situation.

Self-Review

After applying an influence technique, reflect on your intentions and results.

Ethical Simulations

Create fictional scenarios and practice influencing ethically while seeking constructive feedback.

Personal Ethics Code

Write your personal guidelines on how to use dark psychology techniques responsibly.

The Benefits of Ethical Approaches

Lasting Trust

People influenced ethically are more likely to maintain healthy and positive relationships with you.

Solid Reputation

Ethical practice reinforces your credibility and professional image.

Personal and Professional Growth

Ethical approaches promote learning, reflection, and self-development.

The Connection to Dark Psychology

While dark psychology offers powerful tools, ethical application is what distinguishes a skilled strategist from an irresponsible manipulator. Acting with integrity strengthens your influence, enabling you to achieve your goals while fostering healthy and respectful relationships.

Mastering ethics in dark psychology is as important as mastering the techniques themselves. By understanding and respecting boundaries, you transform influence into a force for good, creating a positive and lasting impact in your life and the lives of others.

Chapter 54
Case Studies

Theory without practice is like a map without the corresponding territory. This chapter presents case studies that illustrate the real-world application of the concepts and techniques of dark psychology discussed throughout the book. Through detailed examples, readers can understand how these strategies have been used in various contexts, analyze their implications, and identify important lessons for ethical and effective practice.

The Importance of Case Studies

Deep Understanding

Real-life cases allow visualization of how the techniques work in practice, making the concepts more tangible.

Pattern Recognition

Analyzing multiple cases helps identify recurring trends and strategies.

Ethical Reflection

By studying the consequences of each situation, readers develop a clearer sense of responsibility.

Development of Practical Skills

Analytical practice enhances the ability to apply techniques effectively and ethically.

Case Study 1: Social Manipulation in a Corporate Context

Scenario:

A manager at a tech company aims to implement operational changes but faces resistance from the team. He uses persuasion techniques, strategic communication, and credibility-building to achieve his goals.

Techniques Used:

Rapport and Mirroring

The manager builds a close relationship with influential team members by mirroring their body language and communication style.

Social Proof

He shares examples of other teams that successfully implemented similar changes.

Appeal to Authority

Presents industry experts' data to reinforce the need for change.

Conflict Management

Actively listens to the team's concerns and provides tailored solutions to mitigate objections.

Outcome:

The changes are successfully implemented, initial resistance decreases, and the team adopts the new practices as part of their routine.

Lessons Learned:

Building trust and credibility is essential to overcoming initial barriers.

Personalizing solutions increases acceptance within resistant groups.

Case Study 2: Gaslighting in Personal Relationships

Scenario:

In a personal relationship, one party uses gaslighting to distort the other's perception of reality, undermining their self-confidence and creating emotional dependency.

Techniques Used:

Reality Distortion

The person consistently denies past events or minimizes their partner's concerns.

Social Isolation

Gradually discourages the partner from contacting friends and family, increasing control.

Strategic Guilt

Makes the partner feel guilty for expressing doubts or disagreements.

Outcome:

The affected partner begins to doubt their perceptions, becoming more emotionally dependent on the manipulator.

Lessons Learned:

Gaslighting is a highly destructive technique that can seriously compromise mental health.

Recognizing early signs is crucial to preventing long-term damage.

Case Study 3: Using Scarcity Psychology in Digital Marketing

Scenario:

An online store launches a campaign to promote a new product using scarcity tactics to drive sales.

Techniques Used:

Limited Stock

The store highlights that only 50 units of the product are available.

Countdown Timer

A timer on the product page shows the remaining time for the promotion.

Social Proof

Testimonials and sales figures are displayed to reinforce the product's popularity.

Outcome:

The product sells out in less than 24 hours, and the campaign generates a significant increase in website traffic.

Lessons Learned:

Scarcity triggers psychological urgency that drives action.

Combining social proof with limitations creates a sense of exclusivity.

Case Study 4: Narrative Control in Public Crises

Scenario:

A food company faces criticism on social media after quality issues are discovered in its products. To protect its reputation, the organization implements a narrative control strategy.

Techniques Used:

Controlled Admission

The company acknowledges errors but emphasizes that they are isolated cases.

Focus Redirection

Highlights recent efforts to improve quality and launches charity campaigns to shift attention.

Proactive Engagement

Responds promptly to negative comments, showing empathy and commitment to solutions.

Outcome:

While the initial criticism caused damage, the strategy successfully reverses part of the public opinion, gradually rebuilding consumer trust.

Lessons Learned:

Admitting mistakes transparently can mitigate damage during public crises.

Redirecting attention to positive actions helps balance negative perceptions.

How to Analyze and Apply Case Studies

Identify the Techniques

List the dark psychology tactics employed in the case.

Evaluate the Results

Analyze whether the objectives were achieved and the factors that contributed to success or failure.

Consider Ethics

Determine whether the techniques were used responsibly or manipulatively.

Extract Relevant Lessons

Relate the insights to your own goals and contexts.

Exercises to Practice with Case Studies

Scenario Creation

Develop your own fictional cases to apply the techniques learned.

Review Real-Life Examples

Analyze public events or well-known stories to identify underlying psychological tactics.

Group Discussion

Share and debate cases with others, exploring ethical and strategic perspectives.

Ethics in Case Study Analysis

Studying real cases is a valuable learning tool, but it is essential to approach these situations with respect for ethical implications and the dignity of those involved.

Use examples to learn, not to exploit or justify harmful behavior.

Critically analyze the morality of each action and seek ethical alternatives.

The Connection to Dark Psychology

Case studies consolidate theoretical knowledge and enhance practical understanding of dark psychology techniques. They demonstrate how these tactics can be used to influence, solve problems, or face challenges while highlighting the ethical boundaries necessary for responsible application.

Mastering case analysis strengthens strategic skills, enabling you to exert influence effectively and conscientiously.

Chapter 55
Practices and Exercises

Theory becomes practical skill when applied consistently and strategically. This chapter offers a comprehensive collection of exercises and practices designed to reinforce the concepts and techniques presented throughout this book. Through repetition and adaptation of these activities to your personal context, you will be able to integrate the principles of dark psychology into your influence repertoire, always maintaining a focus on ethics and purpose.

The Importance of Practice in Dark Psychology

Skill Development

Consistent practice allows you to refine your techniques and enhance their application in real-world scenarios.

Strengthening Intuition

Repetition helps internalize patterns and principles, enabling quick and effective responses in complex situations.

Building Confidence

Practice reduces uncertainty and increases your confidence in using influence strategies.

Adapting to Varied Contexts

Simulations and exercises expand your ability to adjust approaches based on different situations.

Exercises to Refine Communication

Body Language Practice

Stand in front of a mirror and observe your posture, gestures, and facial expressions. Adjust to convey confidence and openness.

Record your interactions and analyze how your body language complements or contradicts your words.

Mirroring Techniques

During casual conversations, subtly mirror the other person's posture, gestures, and tone of voice.

Evaluate how this affects the interaction dynamic and the level of connection created.

Voice Tone Control

Practice vocal modulations, such as softening or intensifying your tone, to convey specific emotions.

Use recordings to compare variations and identify their impact in different contexts.

Narrative Development

Create short stories based on personal experiences, emphasizing emotions and lessons learned.

Share these stories with friends or colleagues and request feedback on the emotional impact.

Activities for Behavior Reading

Public Observation

In busy places, observe interactions between people and identify body language signals such as tension, relaxation, or interest.

Try predicting people's moods or intentions based on their expressions and gestures.

Microexpression Analysis

Use videos of interviews or speeches to identify subtle changes in speakers' facial expressions.

Compare your observations with verbal content to assess emotional congruence.

Reaction Simulation

Ask a friend to simulate specific emotions, such as surprise or distrust, while you try to identify them.

Discuss the observed signals to improve your accuracy.

Exercises for Building Rapport

Active Listening

During conversations, practice listening without interrupting, reflecting key points to demonstrate understanding.

Observe how this approach improves connection and the other person's receptiveness.

Open-Ended Questions

Ask questions that encourage detailed responses, deepening your understanding of the other person's needs and perspectives.

Quick Connection Exercise

In brief interactions, aim to create a positive impression through smiles, friendly gestures, and relevant comments.

Evaluate the other person's response and adjust your approach accordingly.

Tactics to Refine Persuasion Techniques

Negotiation Simulations

Participate in negotiation games with friends, applying principles such as anchoring and reciprocity.

Record the impact of different strategies and refine your approach based on results.

Decision-Making Scenarios

Create fictional scenarios to test how different persuasion tactics influence choices.

Example: Offer product or service options and experiment with using social proof or scarcity to motivate decisions.

Feedback Exercise

Work in real situations, such as requesting favors or proposing ideas, applying subtle persuasion techniques.

Request feedback on how your approaches were perceived and adjust as necessary.

Training for Recognizing and Resisting Manipulation

Advertising Campaign Analysis

Examine advertisements or digital campaigns to identify influence tactics, such as emotional appeals or scarcity.

Discuss with friends or colleagues how these techniques affect decisions.

Manipulative Scenario Simulation

Work with a partner to create fictional manipulative situations, identifying signs and strategies for resistance.

Counter-Narrative Development

When confronted with a persuasive narrative, practice crafting a response that challenges or redirects the message.

Internal Reflection Exercise

After social or professional interactions, reflect on how you reacted to influences and how you could adjust your responses.

How to Integrate Practices into Daily Life

Set Weekly Goals

Define specific objectives, such as improving a persuasion technique or identifying manipulation signals.

Document Your Progress

Keep a journal to record your experiences, insights, and areas for improvement.

Seek Regular Feedback

Ask trusted individuals to evaluate how your influence skills evolve over time.

Combine Theory and Practice

Review previous chapters of the book while applying the concepts in real-life scenarios.

Ethics in the Practice of Dark Psychology

All practices and exercises must be conducted responsibly and respectfully:

Use your skills to foster authentic connections and constructive solutions.

Avoid exploiting vulnerabilities or influencing decisions against others' interests.

The Connection to Dark Psychology

This chapter is a crucial step in transforming theoretical knowledge into practical skills. Consistent practice will enable you to master the techniques presented throughout the book, adapting them to your unique goals and contexts.

By applying these practices, you will solidify your ability to exercise influence strategically, ethically, and effectively, becoming a skilled communicator and negotiator ready to face real-world challenges.

Chapter 56
Conclusion and Next Steps

The journey through dark psychology has unveiled a vast universe of techniques, strategies, and concepts that, when used ethically and consciously, can transform the way you interact with the world around you. This chapter serves as a final reflection on the knowledge gained, a review of the key topics covered, and practical guidance for continuing to explore and apply this knowledge responsibly.

Reflection on the Journey

Throughout the chapters, you have delved into topics ranging from the fundamentals of dark psychology to advanced techniques of influence and self-protection. This knowledge has provided you with:

Self-Awareness

A deeper understanding of your own motivations, emotions, and behaviors.

Social Understanding

The ability to interpret the thoughts, intentions, and actions of others with greater accuracy.

Influence Tools

Practical strategies to shape behaviors, build connections, and achieve goals.

Psychological Resilience

Techniques to protect yourself from external manipulations while maintaining your autonomy and integrity.

Review of Key Concepts

The Essence of Dark Psychology

The ability to understand and influence human vulnerabilities without compromising ethical values.

Fundamentals of Influence

Persuasion, manipulation, and effective communication are fundamental pillars of dark psychology.

Behavioral Reading

The identification of emotional cues and body language patterns to uncover hidden intentions.

Advanced Techniques

Approaches such as gaslighting, narrative control, and conversational hypnosis illustrate the power and complexity of dark psychology.

Ethics and Responsibility

Conscious and responsible use of these skills is essential to prevent harm and foster mutual benefits.

Practical Application of Knowledge

Set Clear Goals

Identify specific areas where you want to apply the concepts learned, such as interpersonal communication, leadership, or negotiations.

Practice Regularly

Apply the techniques in everyday situations, evaluate their effects, and adjust your approaches.

Monitor Your Actions

Reflect on your intentions and impacts, ensuring that your practices align with your values.

Seek Feedback

Consult trusted individuals to assess how your actions and influences are perceived.

Expand Your Knowledge

Continue exploring related topics such as emotional intelligence, leadership, and behavioral psychology.

Future Challenges and How to Overcome Them

Recognizing Limits

Balancing influence and manipulation requires self-awareness and self-control.

Keeping Up with Social Changes
The dynamics of influence are constantly evolving; stay updated with new research and trends.

Resisting External Manipulations
Continuously strengthen your mental and emotional resilience to guard against unethical influences.

Exploring New Paths
Dark psychology is only one piece of the puzzle of human behavior. Consider broadening your understanding through:

Positive Psychology
Explore how to foster well-being and personal growth in your interactions.

Emotional Intelligence
Develop skills to manage emotions and build deeper connections.

Advanced Studies in Communication
Delve deeper into linguistics, semiotics, and discourse analysis to refine your influence further.

Ethical Guidelines for the Future
As you continue applying the concepts of dark psychology, remember that true power lies in responsibility. To ensure your impact remains positive:

Respect Autonomy
Do not manipulate or coerce others into making decisions against their will.

Promote Mutual Benefits
Ensure that your actions create value for all parties involved.

Learn from Your Experiences
Reflect on mistakes and successes to continually refine your approach.

Connection to a Greater Purpose
Dark psychology, as explored in this book, is not merely a set of manipulation tools. It is a lens to understand the complexity of human behavior while inviting introspection.

By mastering these techniques, you place yourself in a unique position to:

Navigate social interactions with confidence and clarity.

Protect yourself from external influences while preserving your authenticity.

Inspire and lead ethically, building lasting and meaningful relationships.

The Next Step

With this knowledge in hand, you are prepared to explore new horizons, both personally and professionally. Continue learning, practicing, and growing, transforming your life and the lives of others through positive and intentional influence.

Your journey through dark psychology does not end here. This is merely the beginning of a path where the power of human understanding becomes the key to achieving greater goals, always with integrity and purpose.

Epilogue

As you reach the end of this journey, you realize that the true wealth of knowledge lies in the transformation it brings. Each concept explored, each technique unveiled, was not just theoretical learning but a lived experience—a discovery of the infinite possibilities of understanding and action within the field of dark psychology.

Yet, the end of a book does not signify the end of learning. On the contrary, it is the starting point for the ideas revealed here to blossom in your everyday life. Looking back on the chapters traversed, you encounter a mosaic of insights, where each piece forms a larger picture: a profound understanding of the forces that govern human interactions.

Dark psychology is not merely a field of study; it is a lens through which we learn to navigate the complexities of the world. Most importantly, it teaches us that the power to influence begins within ourselves. By mastering our emotions and recognizing our own biases and vulnerabilities, we become stronger and more aware of how to interact with others.

Here, at this final point, responsibility meets power. Using what you have learned demands wisdom, ethics, and compassion. Each technique holds the potential to create or destroy, depending on how it is applied. The choice is yours. After all, understanding human motivations should not be a weapon but a bridge—a means to build authentic connections, resolve conflicts, and protect those we care about.

And now, you carry with you a rare knowledge. What will you do with it? This is not a rhetorical question; it is an invitation to action. Transform what you have learned into a tool for personal and collective growth. Let this book be the beginning of a new way of living, where human interactions become both a field of learning and a realm of possibilities.

The journey does not end here. It continues with every decision you make, every person you meet, and every choice you make to shape the world around you. The cycle completes itself, but the story is just beginning. The next chapter is yours to write.

www.ingramcontent.com/pod-product-compliance
Lightning Source LLC
LaVergne TN
LVHW040044080526
838202LV00045B/3482